100 - 374183 -A

Section 2

268

PUZZLE from a HOLIDAY ISLE

Did her host hope to marry

The Maclean children . . . from last Friday's Daily Express.

MRS. MACLEAN?

I HAD not been back in London from my summer holiday in Minorca more than a few days when the Mrs. Maclean story broke, and almost before you could say Melinda there I was in the air headed back for the Balearic Islands again.

This time I was off to Majorca, where Mrs. Maclean, her mother, and her three small children had spent August and the first part of September.

Actual spot where the Maclean family stayed was about as far from the noisy, over-full capital of Palma as you could get—Cala Ratjada, 60 miles distant on the mountainous, lovely eastern coast.

This place C.R. is a favourite with moneyed Americans of the type who usually go to Florida in their retirement. The U.S. dollar goes a whole lot further in Majorca (servants cost three pesetas—just over sevenpence.--an hour) and you can live the good life in the sunshine for mighty little by American standards.

So good is the life, indeed, that one local U.S. resident has improved on nature by building a charming swimming pool a few yards from the edge of the sea.

In that pool the Maclean children, Fergus, Donald, and baby Melinda, splashed happily in the golden August days.

by . . . René MacColl

THE GUN-TOTER

'Left shocked'

THE family, including Mrs. Dunbar, Mrs. Maclean's mother, stayed at the villa of widower Douglas MacKillop. MacKillop, a stocky fellow in his late thirties, who sports a brown moustache, and likes to wear rust-coloured shorts, comes from San Francisco.

In the war he was an expert in studying photo-reconnaissance pictures taken by the U.S. Air Force. Afterwards he was gun-toting chief security officer for the Marshall plan people in Paris, making sure that officials locked up their desks at night, and so on.

He was left "shocked, hurt, and bewildered" by Mrs. Maclean's disappearance so soon after she had enjoyed his hospitality, he told me.

Now from this little "away-from-it-all" bathing beach,

RE: DONALD DUART MacLEAN,
ET AL. ESPIONAGE-R.

Cambridge Five Spy Ring, Part 8 of 42

The Federal Bureau of Investigation (FBI)

The BiblioGov Project is an effort to expand awareness of the public documents and records of the U.S. Government via print publications. In broadening the public understanding of government and its work, an enlightened democracy can grow and prosper. Ranging from historic Congressional Bills to the most recent Budget of the United States Government, the BiblioGov Project spans a wealth of government information. These works are now made available through an environmentally friendly, print-on-demand basis, using only what is necessary to meet the required demands of an interested public. We invite you to learn of the records of the U.S. Government, heightening the knowledge and debate that can lead from such publications.

Included are the following Collections:

Budget of The United States Government
Presidential Documents
United States Code
Education Reports from ERIC
GAO Reports
History of Bills
House Rules and Manual
Public and Private Laws

Code of Federal Regulations
Congressional Documents
Economic Indicators
Federal Register
Government Manuals
House Journal
Privacy act Issuances
Statutes at Large

rowsing happily in the sun, and wakened only occasionally by the roar of luxury speedboats, I switch the scene to the interior of the crowded plane in which I am again flying back to London, by way of Barcelona and Paris.

Our old friend the Long Arm of Coincidence rarely taps me on the shoulder, but this is what happened. I am filling in one of those official cards that one is always filling in as one flies about Europe, when the snappily dressed young man sitting beside me squints down at it and says: "René MacColl! My Paris friends often talk about you. How do you do?"

Turns out he is an American named Harrison Elliott, who runs a business in Paris, and that we have mutual friends from my days as Paris chief reporter.

'DOUGLAS?'

—His old friend

WE talk of this and that. The Maclean case comes up. I tell him I've just been in Majorca on it. Where was Mrs. Maclean staying down there? "At the house of a chap called Douglas MacKillop." I say. Whereupon Elliott chokes on the peach which he is in process of eating as dessert to the airline lunch, gives out a loud strangled cry, and proceeds as follows: "Douglas MacKillop! But he is one of my oldest friends. Known him for years. I come from San Francisco too.

"But this is extraordinary. About the last thing Douglas said to my wife and me before he left Paris for Majorca last summer was 'I hope to get married while I am in Majorca.'

"We couldn't figure that out. Douglas lost his first wife about a year ago and he was lonely. But Cala Ratjada is about the last place in the world you would go if you wanted to meet a possible new wife casually."

(I can confirm that. Eligible single women down there are as rare as portraits of Malenkov. The U.S. "colony" is almost 100 per cent married couples.)

"Douglas wrote me many letters, but the funny thing is that when I wrote in August asking if my wife and I could go and stay with him, he wrote back saying he was sorry but that "a lady, her mother, and her three children" would be staying. The villa would be full.

"Douglas is very fond of children. It was one of his regrets that his first marriage was childless. 'But that 'marriage' remark certainly has us guessing...."

GOOD FRIENDS

For the holidays

SO there we are. It has been stated that Mrs. Maclean aimed at divorcing her husband, Donald, next spring, when he would have been away from her three years. Was there a new romance in the wind?

MacKillop himself told me: "We are just good friends and I wanted to give them all a nice summer holiday."

He first got to know Mrs. Maclean, he added, because her mother was a friend of his first wife. ...

270

Strain on Intelligence . . . . . By Marquis Childs

Beria Is Case in Point

ANYTHING can happen in the times in which we live. No headline is too fantastic to gain at least momentary acceptance. The "escape" of Lavrenti Beria is a case in point.

Top intelligence authorities in Washington are extremely skeptical about the reports that Beria eluded his enemies in Soviet Russia and is now somewhere in this hemisphere. The latest report puts him in Mexico prepared to offer through a contact man his vast store of secrets in return for asylum in the United States.

The officials who should know about Beria's presence somewhere south of the border do not flatly say the report is untrue for precisely the reason that despite the far-lung resources of the Central Intelligence Agency and the military intelligence services it could be true. But they will be surprised and embarrassed if Beria is produced by a Senate committee. The guess—it is only that— is that he is still alive in a Moscow prison despite the reports that he was killed during an armed revolt in the Kremlin following Stalin's death.

A KNOWN FACT which is at present giving intelligence agencies throughout the West much more concern is the disappearance of Mrs. Melinda MacLean and her three children. She is the American-born wife of Donald MacLean who disappeared more than two years ago in the company of Guy Buurgess. MacLean was an erratic but trusted official of the British foreign office. Burgess had been dismissed following his eccentric behavior while serving in the British Embassy in Washington. Both men left England on a channel boat for France and then vanished, the conjecture being that they went behind the Iron Curtain.

It is assumed that Mrs. MacLean has joined her husband. But coming just when it does, this second walkout is having serious repercussions.

A long-standing complaint from the American side is that British security regulations are too lax. As proof, Klaus Fuchs worked at Britain's top secret atomic center until American authorities provided proof of his treachery. Bruno Pontecorvo, another top atomic physicist, walked out with his family and is presumably working for the Soviets in Russia.

These dramatic episodes understandably prejudiced American opinion against relaxation of laws that now forbid the exchange of atomic information with the British. In Congress they stirred a strong conviction that the present barriers must be maintained.

Yet policy-makers on both sides of the Atlantic are increasingly aware of how much this barrier of secrecy costs. The British will shortly conduct a new series of atomic tests on the Woomera range in Australia. These will repeat to some extent steps already taken by the Atomic Energy Commission. And it is obvious that if Britain could avoid following the same costly road, there would be more money and material available for the defense of western Europe.

ANOTHER and more serious aspect of the secrecy barrier is the fact that military planning in the North Atlantic Treaty Organization cannot be based on realistic knowledge of the kind and the number of atomic weapons available. A large empty space must be left on the tables of organization which means that European commanders cannot be sure whether too much or too little emphasis is being placed on ground forces and other conventional defenses.

Hope has risen for changes in the present restrictions. And then just as proposals were being worked out which the White House would take up with congressional leaders, Mrs. MacLean drops out of sight.

American intelligence authorities long experienced in the cloak and dagger trade are inclined to be sympathetic with their opposite numbers in British intelligence. They point out that Mrs. MacLean was living in Switzerland. It is difficult particularly in a neutral country to keep a constant watch on an individual free to get into her own car and go anywhere she wants to.

Current conjectures are these. Mrs. MacLean was persuaded by a plausible Soviet agent that her husband was in the Soviet zone of Austria and he begged only for a brief visit with her and the children, the youngest of whom he had never seen. Once in the zone, she was, of course, seized. A second theory is much simpler —that in response to a direct and verifiable appeal from her husband, she elected to join him in exile. And the rest, short of some wholly unexpected upheaval, is almost certain to be the same sinister silence that has closed in around the others.

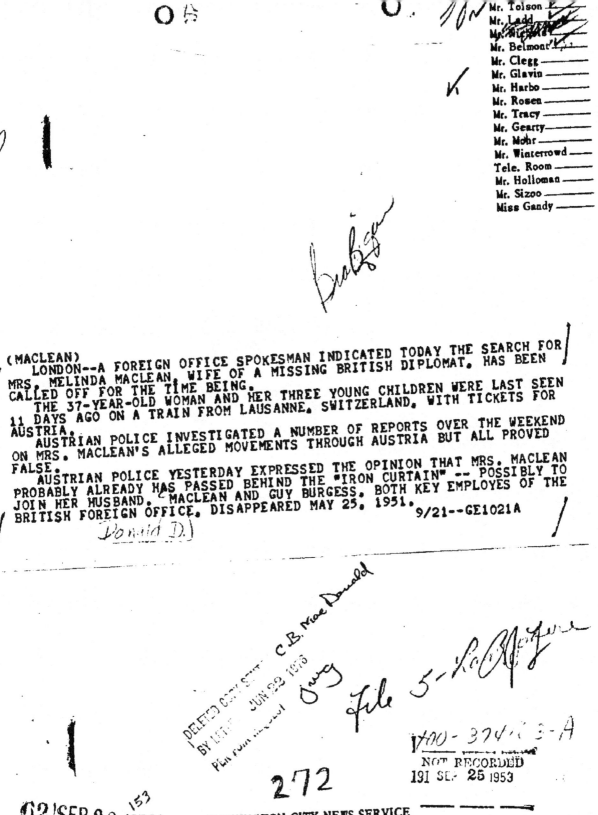

(MACLEAN)

LONDON--A FOREIGN OFFICE SPOKESMAN INDICATED TODAY THE SEARCH FOR MRS. MELINDA MACLEAN, WIFE OF A MISSING BRITISH DIPLOMAT, HAS BEEN CALLED OFF FOR THE TIME BEING.

THE 37-YEAR-OLD WOMAN AND HER THREE YOUNG CHILDREN WERE LAST SEEN 11 DAYS AGO ON A TRAIN FROM LAUSANNE, SWITZERLAND, WITH TICKETS FOR AUSTRIA.

AUSTRIAN POLICE INVESTIGATED A NUMBER OF REPORTS OVER THE WEEKEND ON MRS. MACLEAN'S ALLEGED MOVEMENTS THROUGH AUSTRIA BUT ALL PROVED FALSE.

AUSTRIAN POLICE YESTERDAY EXPRESSED THE OPINION THAT MRS. MACLEAN PROBABLY ALREADY HAS PASSED BEHIND THE "IRON CURTAIN" -- POSSIBLY TO JOIN HER HUSBAND. MACLEAN AND GUY BURGESS, BOTH KEY EMPLOYES OF THE BRITISH FOREIGN OFFICE, DISAPPEARED MAY 25, 1951. 9/21--GE1021A

272

NOT RECORDED
191 SEP 25 1953

02 SEP 28 1953

A love-story to touch our hearts—OR WAS IT?

DONALD and Melinda—is this the greatest love story ever told? Some would have us believe it is. Mrs. Dunbar, Melinda's mother, for one.

She provided many of the facts in the brilliant account of the Maclean case recently published in the News Chronicle. And the tone of the articles was strongly sympathetic to Melinda.

No doubt Geoffrey Hoare, who wrote the articles, believes in the love story. Many others believe in it also.

Perhaps they are right. A case supporting the love story can be made out.

RE: DONALD DUART MacLEAN, et al
ESPIONAGE - R
(Bufile 100-374183)

SUNDAY EXPRESS
SEPTEMBER 19, 1954
LONDON, ENGLAND

OFFICE OF THE LEGAL ATTACHE
AMERICAN EMBASSY
LONDON, ENGLAND

100- 37 4183 - A
NOT RECORDED
76 OCT 6 1954

273

On that May evening in 1951 when Donald disappeared Melinda had two children, Fergus, aged 7, and Donald, 5. They had both been born by Caesarian section. The third baby was due in a few weeks—on June 14.

This fact alone shows an extraordinary devotion and love for her husband. Few women would look forward, after two difficult births demanding an operation, to a third child which would have to be born the same way.

In contrast is Donald's behaviour towards his slim American wife. His strange character was always most noticeable in his relationship with her.

Meekness

VERY often — and particularly during her pregnancy—the immaculate Foreign Office departmental head would not catch the 5.19 from Victoria to dine with his wife and play with his children.

He stayed in London and she did not hear from him for two or three days. Sometimes he was drunk. Sometimes he preferred the company of his friends. Few women would put up with such behaviour.

But apparently Melinda bore it with a meekness that would have surprised an Early Victorian housewife.

This was the situation on the eve of Donald's 38th birthday in May 1951, when he suddenly announced he would bring a friend home to dinner. In spite of her condition and of his odd behaviour she set about making him a birthday cake. The friend was Burgess. He left after dinner at nine o'clock. He went to Southampton with Burgess and disappeared behind the Iron Curtain.

by JOHN DEANE POTTER

Obedient

WHEN he left there is now no question that Donald was confident of his wife's unswerving love and obedience. For events have shown that he felt he could depend upon her unquestioning devotion to receive secret messages from him, however mystifying they were and however sinister the methods he used to get in touch with her.

Obviously he never thought for a moment she would question his motives or betray his whereabouts or the contact men his friends employed.

How much that confidence was justified! Even to her mother, who was her closest confidante apart from her husband, she never uttered one word which would give any clue to her missing husband's secret.

She took a flat in Geneva to be ready when the word came to join him. In a letter, according to Geoffrey Hoare, she said: "This is the first time I have lived in the middle of a city for years, and I simply love it. Never mention the country to me again except for week-ends or holidays."

But did she really love it because in the anonymity of a big city it was possible to receive messages without anyone interfering with her plans to join her husband?

When the call came she obeyed it unhesitatingly. She bought her new daughter Pink Rose a new coat and shoes to meet the father she had never seen.

Overnight she renounced everything she had known, believed, and had been brought up with.

She left her mother without a goodbye or a backward glance. She must have known she might never see her again.

Was it because of her love for him that she took her children to join their father? Was it because of that love that she crossed the frontier that divides the world into two without a sigh of farewell? If so, it is the story of a wife's devotion unparalleled in modern history.

But is it convincing? Or has Mrs. Dunbar mistaken the motives of her own daughter?

There could be a stronger and stranger motive for the behaviour of Melinda.

The student

GO back to the crowded, cosmopolitan Café Flore on the Left Bank in Paris at Christmas 1939. It was there during the period of the phoney war that Melinda was introduced to Donald.

He was good looking and 26, a Foreign Office man who would perhaps be an ambassador one day.

She was a 23-year-old American girl who had spent a year in Paris studying in a desultory way at the Sorbonne.

It was a significant moment in Western Europe. At that time Communism among the intellectuals had probably reached its highest peak. The Spanish Civil War, with its fiercely felt political chasms, was not far behind. The Left Bank cafés were filled with refugees from Fascism. Anti-Hitlerism had given Communism an impetus it has never since enjoyed in the free world.

And Melinda talked and sat with the fluent advocates of international Communism day after day until two or three o'clock in the morning in the crowded chair-to-chair cafés of St. Germain des Pres.

It would have been impossible, unless she were deaf, not to hear their dogma repeated nearly every minute.

Did she absorb it?

274

from Nazism and the talk of their café Communist friends had left a mark on both of them which they could never erase? Particularly as it happened at the most impressionable time of their lives—the time of the war and their youthful marriage.

Was she a victim of what George Orwell called the double-think—the ability to present an impeccable British diplomatic countenance to the world, while underneath, renouncing everything it stood for?

There is no doubt now that is what Donald did.

How far did his wife know what he was doing?

How else, except by sympathy for his beliefs, can some of her actions be explained?

She obviously received messages from him apart from the £2,000 which was paid into Swiss banks for her.

Look at the evidence disclosed by Hoare. In May last year, four months before she disappeared, she had passport photographs taken of her three children in the name of Smith.

Little Fergus watching another child playing with soldiers, said: "My daddy is fighting for peace." Could anyone but his mother have told him that?

The wife

SHE married Donald in 1940 while the German guns muttered ominously outside Paris. They spent their honeymoon in a field with other refugees fleeing from conquered Paris before being taken by boat from Bordeaux back to England. Could it be that their flight

Bewildered

AGAIN, according to Geoffrey Hoare, M.I.5 put it to her quite bluntly, in an interview with her after Donald's disappearance, that she knew he was a Communist—also that she was probably a Communist herself and was planning to join him. Melinda professed great bewilderment and indignation at this at the time.

But in fact she did join him, just as they suspected she would.

On that May night in 1951 did Donald tell her the game was up? Had he been warned that the authorities knew he was a traitor?

Well-informed friends of mine in Washington believe that in fact some people in the British Foreign Office looked the other way while Donald Maclean fled, glad to be rid of a senior official who might cause one of the greatest international sensations ever known. They further believe the F.B.I. stumbled across a link with him in the course of their anti-Red investigations.

Her decision

SOMEHOW Maclean may have found out about this.

If Melinda shared his political views how much easier and understandable her decision to join him would be.

There would be no unbearable remorse at leaving her mother.

There would be no pangs at renouncing Britain, the land of her marriage, and America, the land of her birth.

There would be no tears at the prospect of taking her three children to a foreign land where they will always be at a disadvantage and will for ever bear the stigma of their parents' misconduct.

Can her decision in fact be understood except as a deliberate choice to bring them up as Communists? Can her secret flight be explained save on political grounds?

The real answer is unknown. But the argument continues.

Is Melinda as much of a Communist as her husband? Was she perhaps the mainspring of his actions all along? Or is this, after all, the greatest love story ever told?

275

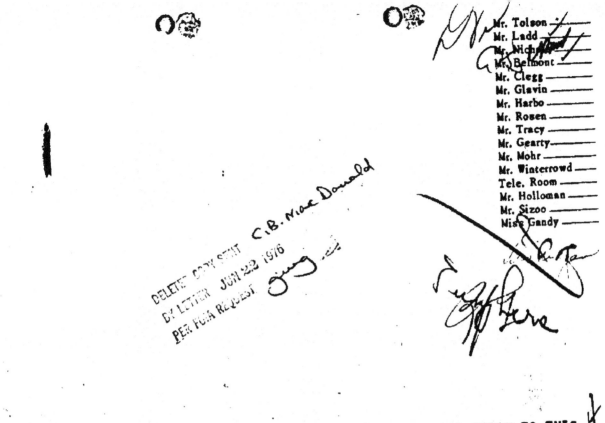

DELETED COPY SENT C.B. MacDonald
BY LETTER JUN 22 1976
PER FOIA REQUEST

(MACLEAN)
VIENNA -- THE SEARCH FOR MRS. MELINDA MACLEAN SWITCHED TODAY TO THIS DIVIDED CITY OF INTERNATIONAL INTRIGUE WHERE SHE COULD EASILY HAVE CROSSED THE IRON CURTAIN -- POSSIBLY TO JOIN HER LONG-MISSING BRITISH DIPLOMAT HUSBAND.

THE 37-YEAR-OLD AMERICAN-BORN WOMAN AND HER THREE YOUNG CHILDREN WERE LAST SEEN ON A TRAIN LEAVING LAUSANNE, SWITZERLAND, WITH TICKETS FOR AUSTRIA A WEEK AGO FRIDAY. THEIR TRAIL HAS TURNED COLD BY NOW.

BRITISH AUTHORITIES ASKED THE "URGENT ASSISTANCE" OF AUSTRIAN POLICE IN TRACING THEIR MOVEMENTS.

IN LONDON, THE NEWSPAPER DAILY MAIL OFFERED $28,000 REWARD FOR EVIDENCE OF THE WHEREABOUTS OF THE MACLEANS "WHETHER OR NOT THEY ARE ACTUALLY FREE AGENTS." THE DAILY EXPRESS OFFERED $5,600.

BUT THEIR DISAPPEARANCE SEEMED DESTINED TO TURN INTO ANOTHER DRAMATIC CHAPTER IN ONE OF THE MOST INTRIGUING MYSTERIES OF COLD WAR DIPLOMACY.

AUTHORITIES HAD NO MORE HOPE OF SOLVING THIS PHASE THAN THEY DID THE MYSTERY OF DONALD D. MACLEAN AND GUY BURGESS, KEY EMPLOYES OF THE BRITISH FOREIGN OFFICE WHO DISAPPEARED MAY 25, 1951.

THE PREVALENT THEORY IS THE TWO DIPLOMATS ARE BEHIND THE IRON CURTAIN. MACLEAN WAS HEAD OF THE AMERICAN DEPARTMENT OF THE BRITISH FOREIGN OFFICE AND BURGESS WAS AN EXPERT ON MARXISM. 9/19--MJ940A

David Lawrence—

Internal Security Test in Britain

Donald Maclean Disappeared Behind the Iron Curtain With Secret Data, and Now His Wife Has Vanished

Donald Maclean—a British official, known among his friends as a Communist—in some strange way eluded the British security services in May, 1951, and disappeared behind the Iron Curtain bearing confidential information he had been accumulating from his intimate contacts with the governments of the United States and Great Britain.

Now his American-born wife has disappeared under circumstances equally mysterious, and the world is wondering whether the British security service fell down again on whether perhaps it now will be in the position to confound its critics by exposing the whole story and revealing that perhaps it has known all along what was going on.

The latter theory is one that naturally arises wishfully among those familiar with intelligence work. For it would be incredible if the British security service, knowing how important it was to obtain every scrap of information about the whereabouts of Maclean and his associate, Guy Burgess, would fail to shadow the family in Switzerland and keep in touch with every one who might seek to talk with the wife of the missing diplomat.

Certainly if the intelligence agents have been and are still on the job, it may be days before they will discover the place where Messrs. Maclean and Burgess have been hiding. There would certainly have been no point in intercepting Mrs. Maclean but it would be shrewd rather to maintain uninterrupted surveillance until it could be determined exactly where she was headed.

Why is the whole episode important? It's because Donald Maclean served as a secretary of the British Embassy in Washington along with another secretary, Guy Burgess, and the main job of Maclean was to keep in touch with atomic energy developments here. He was secretary of a committee of the allies, including the British government, and was therefore accepted and trusted as a thoroughly reliable person.

When Maclean disappeared and one of the reporters here told former Secretary of State Acheson about it, the latter is reported to have exclaimed: "My God, he knew everything!"

Maclean not only knew about atomic energy matters when he was in America, but at the time of his disappearance he had been given charge of the so-called "American desk" in the British Foreign Office in London. This is the desk over which flows daily all the confidential messages from diplomatic representatives of Great Britain in the United States. Naturally at that time there were very secret exchanges between our State Department and Great Britain relative to plans for ending the Korean war, and there were also objections by the British to the continuance of the conflict if it involved extension of hostilities into Manchuria.

Whatever the information was that the British government had from its close friend and ally, the United States, Donald Maclean was in a position to carry to the Communists. There are various rumors that the Federal Bureau of Investigation here originally had a tip on Maclean's activities and had so notified the British government and that the British security authorities were about to pounce on Maclean and Burgess just as they made their get-away.

Both Maclean and Burgess were college men and were known as brilliant "intellectuals" in literary circles. Their sympathies for Communist doctrine were not difficult to determine, but the British Foreign Office, which was poohpoohing American concern over the Alger Hiss case and the infiltration of other Communists in the State Department, didn't seem to be vigilant in doing a check-up job in the matter of loyalty—any more than it had been when "clearing" Klaus Fuchs for admission to the American atomic energy project.

Whether Mrs. Maclean has gone to see her husband voluntarily or involuntarily, the fact remains that the oft-distributed story from some London sources that Maclean and Burgess had been somehow "liquidated" doesn't seem plausible now any more than the first unofficial intimation that they had just gone on a "holiday binge."

It will be important for the British security service to re-establish faith in its efficiency by getting all the facts, and maybe that's what they have been doing these last few days and some day will reveal. American officials are much concerned, because again the subject of an exchange of atomic secrets with Britain is up for consideration, and Congress is not likely to amend existing law to provide a freer interchange if British security methods are believed to be lax.

(Reproduction Rights Reserved.)

Mr. Tolson
Mr. Ladd
Mr. _____
Mr. Belmont
Mr. Clegg
Mr. Glavin
Mr. Harbo
Mr. Rosen
Mr. Tracy
Mr. Gearty
Mr. Mohr
Mr. Winterrowd
Tele. Room
Mr. Holloman
Mr. Sizoo
Miss Gandy

Donald Duart Maclean

(MACLEAN)
GENEVA, SWITZERLAND--EVIDENCE MOUNTED TODAY THAT MRS. MELINDA MACLEAN KEPT A RENDEZVOUS BEHIND THE IRON CURTAIN WITH HER LONG-MISSING BRITISH DIPLOMAT HUSBAND, BUT POLICE WATCHED A GARAGE WHERE SHE LEFT HER CAR A WEEK AGO SAYING SHE WOULD RETURN FOR IT TODAY.
AT LEAST THREE PERSONS SAID THEY SAW THE 37-YEAR-OLD AMERICAN-BORN MOTHER AND HER THREE CHILDREN ABOARD A TRAIN THAT LEFT LAUSANNE LAST FRIDAY FOR ZURICH.
SWISS POLICE BELIEVED SHE WAS HEADED FOR THE SOVIET ZONE OF AUSTRIA WHEN SHE VANISHED BECAUSE THE TRAIN MAKES EXCELLENT CONNECTIONS WITH AN EXPRESS TO VIENNA AT ZURICH. INSPECTION OF THE EXPRESS AT THE SWISS-AUSTRIAN BORDER IS "ONLY CURSORY," THEY ADDED.
THE SWISS POLICE INTELLIGENCE SERVICE ALSO SAID SHE COULD HAVE TAKEN THE EXPRESS FROM ZURICH TO MILAN TO BETTER COVER HER TRACKS. FROM MILAN SHE COULD HAVE TAKEN THE FAMED ORIENT EXPRESS EASTWARD.
9/18--GE912A

1/11-374182-A
NOT RECORDED
191 SEP 21 1953
278

Mr. Tolson
Mr. Ladd
Mr. _____
Mr. Belmont
Mr. Clegg
Mr. Glavin
Mr. Harbo
Mr. Rosen
Mr. Tracy
Mr. Gearty
Mr. Mohr
Mr. Winterrowd
Tele. Room
Mr. Holloman
Mr. Sizoo
Miss Gandy

Donald Duart Maclean

DELETED COPY
BY LETTER JUN 23
PER FOIA REQUEST

ADD MACLEAN, GENEVA (637P) SOURCES CLOSE TO THE POLICE SAID OFFICIALS THEORIZED THAT THE MACLEANS WENT TO AUSTRIA BECAUSE THE LAUSANNE TRAIN MAKES AN EXCELLENT CONNECTION FOR VIENNA AT ZURICH, AND THE SWISS-AUSTRIAN BORDER INSPECTION IS "ONLY CURSORY."

LATER, THE FAMILY ISSUED A STATEMENT GIVING DETAILS OF THE DISAPPEARANCE AND EXPRESSING ANXIETY FOR MRS. MACLEAN'S SAFETY.

SIGNED BY J. C. SHEERS, A SON-IN-LAW OF MRS. MELINDA DUNBAR, THE MISSING WOMAN'S MOTHER, THE STATEMENT SAID IN PART:

"LAST FRIDAY, SEPT. 11, MRS. MACLEAN TOLD HER MOTHER, MRS. DUNBAR, SHE HAD MET WHILE SHOPPING AN OLD FRIEND FROM CAIRO NAMED ROBIN MUIR, WHO HAD INVITED HER AND HER CHILDREN TO SPEND THE WEEKEND WITH HIM AND HIS FAMILY AT THEIR VILLA NEAR TERRITET.

"MRS. DUNBAR ASKED MRS. MACLEAN IF SHE MEANT TO TAKE HER LITTLE GIRL WHO IS ONLY 27 MONTHS OLD. MRS. MACLEAN SAID SHE WAS GOING TO TAKE THE LITTLE GIRL, FOR MR. MUIR SAID A BABY NURSE COULD CARE FOR HER."

THE STATEMENT SAID MRS. MACLEAN AND HER THREE CHILDREN LEFT HOME ABOUT 3 P.M. THAT DAY WITH 400 FRANCS AND "AN AMOUNT OF BAGGAGE SUITABLE FOR A COUNTRY WEEKEND."

"THEY WERE TO RETURN SUNDAY EVENING BECAUSE THE TWO BOYS WERE TO ENTER SCHOOL EARLY MONDAY MORNING," THE FAMILY SAID.

WHEN THERE WAS NO WORD FROM MRS. MACLEAN SUNDAY, MRS. DUNBAR WAS ALARMED. SHE FELT THAT HER DAUGHTER WOULD HAVE NOTIFIED HER UNDER ORDINARY CIRCUMSTANCES.

WHEN THERE STILL WAS NO WORD MONDAY MORNING, MRS. DUNBAR NOTIFIED THE BRITISH CONSULATE AND THE FOREIGN OFFICE IN LONDON, ASKING THEIR HELP.

THE FAMILY STATEMENT DENOUNCED AS "ABSOLUTELY FALSE" A TELEGRAM PURPORTEDLY SENT BY MRS. MACLEAN TO HER MOTHER SAYING UNFORSEEN CIRCUMSTANCES HAD DELAYED HER RETURN. THE WORDING WAS CONSIDERED WRONG.

9/17--TS1135P

Feb 5

100-374103

NOT RECORDED
191 SEP 31 1953

279

Mr. Tolson
Mr. Ladd
Mr. Nichols
Mr. Belmont
Mr. Clegg
Mr. Glavin
Mr. Harbo
Mr. Rosen
Mr. Tracy
Mr. Gearty
Mr. Mohr
Mr. Winterrowd
Tele. Room
Mr. Holloman
Mr. Sizoo
Miss Gandy

Donald Duart Maclean

(MCLEAN)
   GENEVA, SWITZERLAND--THE WIFE OF A LONG-MISSING BRITISH DIPLOMAT LEFT HER CAR AT A GARAGE IN LAUSANNE "FOR A WEEK" LAST FRIDAY, WENT INTO A RAILROAD STATION AND VANISHED WITH HER THREE CHILDREN, POLICE LEARNED.
   MRS. MELINDA MACLEAN DEPARTED FROM HER HOME IN GENEVA FRIDAY TO SPEND A WEEK-END WITH A "MR. ROBIN, A FRIEND FROM CAIRO," AT A RESORT ABOUT 50 MILES AWAY. DONALD D. MACLEAN, HER HUSBAND WHO DISAPPEARED MORE THAN TWO YEARS AGO -- POSSIBLY BEHIND THE IRON CURTAIN -- WAS ONCE STATIONED IN THE EGYPTIAN CAPITAL.
   A SEARCH STARTED FOR "MR. ROBIN" AND A MYSTERIOUS "ROUND-FACED" WOMAN WHO SENT A TELEGRAM YESTERDAY IN MRS. MACLEAN'S NAME TO HER MOTHER IN GENEVA SAYING "ALL EXTREMELY WELL."
   9/17--CE837A

C.B. MacDonald

100-374183

DELETED COPY SENT
BY LETTER JUN 22 1970
PER FOIA Request

100-374183 A

NOT RECORDED
191 SEP 21 1953

53 SEP 24 1953

280

WASHINGTON CITY NEWS SERVICE

ADD MACLEAN, GENEVA

THE GARAGE ATTENDANT IDENTIFIED A PHOTOGRAPH OF THE 37-YEAR-OLD AMERICAN-BORN MOTHER AS THE WOMAN WHO DROVE UP IN A 1952 BLACK CHEVROLET WITH HER THREE CHILDREN AND ASKED TO LEAVE THE AUTO FOR A WEEK. HE SAID SHE THEN ENTERED THE NEARBY RAILROAD STATION.

"THE LADY SEEMED EXTREMELY NERVOUS AND IMPATIENT," ATTENDANT MARCEL MICHELI SAID. "AFTERWARD I WATCHED HER AND THE CHILDREN ENTER THE STATION. I NOTICED SHE HAD NO LUGGAGE WHATSOEVER."

POLICE ALSO ANNOUNCED THAT MRS. MACLEAN APPARENTLY DID NOT SEND THE "I'M ALL RIGHT" TELEGRAM WHICH HER MOTHER RECEIVED YESTERDAY AT THE GENEVA HOME WHERE THEY WERE BOTH LIVING.

"A LADY WHO WAS NOT MRS. MACLEAN" FILED THE TELEGRAM FROM THE POST OFFICE AT TERRITET, SWITZERLAND, YESTERDAY FIVE DAYS AFTER MRS. MACLEAN DISAPPEARED, GENEVA POLICE CHIEF CHARLES KNECHT SAID.

WHEN MRS. MACLEAN LEFT GENEVA FRIDAY WITH HER THREE CHILDREN SHE TOLD HER MOTHER SHE WAS GOING TO SPEND THE WEEK-END WITH "A MAN I KNOW" AT TERRITET, A RESORT OUTSIDE MONTREUX AND NEAR LAUSANNE ACROSS LAKE GENEVA FROM GENEVA. THE ADDRESS SHE GAVE FOR THE FRIEND TURNED OUT TO BE NON-EXISTENT.

THE NEW DEVELOPMENTS STRENGTHENED BELIEFS OF DIPLOMATIC OBSERVERS THAT MRS. MACLEAN MAY HAVE GONE TO JOIN HER HUSBAND AT A SECRET RENDEZVOUS -- POSSIBLY BEHIND THE IRON CURTAIN. BUT THERE WAS NO DIRECT EVIDENCE FOR THE THEORY.

THE DISAPPEARANCE OF MRS. MACLEAN, THE FORMER MELINDA MARLING OF NEW YORK AND MASSACHUSETTS, HAS REVIVED AND DEEPEND ONE OF THE BIGGEST MYSTERIES OF COLD WAR DIPLOMACY -- WHAT HAPPENED TO HER HUSBAND, DONALD D. MACLEAN, AND GUY BURGESS, BRITISH FOREIGN OFFICE EMPLOYES WHO VANISHED MAY 25, 1951.

9/17--GE912A

281

Mr. Tolson
Mr. Ladd
Mr. Nichols
Mr. Belmont
Mr. Clegg
Mr. Glavin
Mr. Harbo
Mr. Rosen
Mr. Tracy
Mr. Gearty
Mr. Mohr
Mr. Winterrowd
Tele. Room
Mr. Holloman
Mr. Sizoo
Miss Gandy

BRANIGAN ✓

Donald Duart Maclean

(MACLEAN)

GENEVA--MRS. DONALD MACLEAN, MISSING AMERICAN WIFE OF A MISSING BRITISH DIPLOMAT, BOARDED A TRAIN HEADED TOWARD THE IRON CURTAIN IN LAUSANNE LAST WEEK, POLICE WERE TOLD TODAY.

TWO WITNESSES TOLD POLICE THAT MRS. MACLEAN AND HER THREE CHILDREN LEFT LAUSANNE FRIDAY IN AN EXPRESS TRAIN BOUND FOR ZURICH, WHERE THEY COULD HAVE MADE DIRECT CONNECTIONS WITH A TRAIN BOUND FOR OCCUPIED AUSTRIA.

THE WITNESSES WERE PROF. ANDRE GUIGNARD, OF LAUSANNE UNIVERSITY, AND AN UNIDENTIFIED WOMAN WHO SAID SHE SAW MRS. MACLEAN AND THE CHILDREN SITTING IN A SECOND-CLASS COMPARTMENT ON THE TRAIN.

MRS. MACLEAN, THE FORMER MELINDA MARLING OF NEW YORK CITY, LEFT HER HOME IN GENEVA FRIDAY, OSTENSIBLY TO VISIT "MR. ROBIN, A FRIEND FROM CAIRO," AT A RESORT SOME 50 MILES AWAY.

SHE HAD PREVIOUSLY BEEN TRACED AS FAR AS LAUSANNE, WHERE SHE LEFT HER CAR IN A GARAGE AND VANISHED INTO THE RAILROAD STATION. HER HUSBAND, WHO DISAPPEARED MORE THAN TWO YEARS AGO, IS GENERALLY BELIEVED TO HAVE FLED TO IRON-CURTAIN TERRITORY. 9/17--TS440P

DELETED COPY SENT C.B. MacDonald
BY LETTER
PER FOIA REQUEST

79 SEP 22 1953

100-374183

Feb 6
100-374183-A
NOT RECORDED
191 SEP 21 1953
282

Donald Duart Maclean

ADD MACLEAN, GENEVA (440P)
   GUIGNARD SAID JUST BEFORE THE TRAIN LEFT THE LAUSANNE STATION,
MRS. MACLEAN LOST SIGHT OF HER TWO BOYS AND "SEEMED TO BECOME NEARLY
HYSTERICAL."
   "SHE TURNED AROUND AND STARTED LOOKING WILDLY FOR THEM," HE SAID.
   GUIGNARD SAID THE BOYS DROPPED OUT OF SIGHT MOMENTARILY WHEN THEY
ENTERED THEIR RAILWAY COACH THROUGH A DOOR SOME DISTANCE FROM THEIR
MOTHER.
   "WHEN SHE SAW THEM DISAPPEARING INTO THE OTHER DOOR, SHE KNEW
THEY WERE ALL RIGHT AND CALLED OUT, 'OH, THERE YOU ARE.'" GUIGNARD
SAID.
   9/17--TS637P

DELETED COPY SENT C.B. MacDonald
JUN 22 1976
BY

100-37418 3-11
NOT RECORDED
191 SEP 21 1953

7 9 SEP 22 1953   WASHINGTON CITY NEWS SERVICE

283

WIFE, FAMILY OF 'MISSING' BRITON VANISH

Fear Kidnaping Of MacLeans

GENEVA, Sept. 15 (N.Y. News) —Mrs. Melinda MacLean, American wife of a British diplomat, who mysteriously disappeared two years ago—possibly behind the iron curtain—vanished Tuesday with her three children and police fear they may have been kidnaped.

Their disappearance was re-

MRS. MELINDA MacLEAN

ported by the frantic mother of Mrs. MacLean, Mrs. Melinda G. Dunbar, of New York City. They had been living together at Mrs. Dunbar's Swiss villa.

All border posts, airfield and train and bus termini have been alerted for the MacLeans—the mother and her sons, Fergus, 9, and Donald, 7, and daughter, Melinda, 2. Melinda was born three weeks after her father, Donald MacLean, 38, head of the American department of the British foreign office, vanished from the free world with another British diplomat on May 25, 1951.

Kidnaping Feared

The disappearance of MacLean and Guy Burgess, 40, a specialist in Far Eastern affairs, presented Scotland Yard with one of its greatest mysteries. The British government says to this day it doesn't know where the pair went, or why.

Mrs. Dunbar, on the verge of hysteria after awaiting word from her daughter all day, called in police and said, "They must have been kidnaped."

She said she went for a walk in the morning and, upon returning, found the house empty. She called "everybody we know" without result.

At the time of the disappearance of MacLean and Burgess, 15,000 police and secret agents worked on the case. They traced the pair as far as France, and there the trial ended.

Most British papers speculated that they fled behind the Iron Curtain. Both, and especially Burgess, were known to associate with Communists and other leftists. Burgess had been recalled from Washington only a month before they vanished.

Hoped for Return

A State department spokesman said at the time the two vanished that MacLean was a member of the committee which controled wartime exchanges between the United States and its Allies in developing the atomic bomb.

But Mrs. MacLean, then expecting her third child, felt certain to the end that her husband would reappear. It was only months after Melinda was born that hope started to wane.

It never faded, however. She moved to France, in the Beauvallon region where her husband had been reported sighted. Then, when her money ran out, she stayed briefly in Paris.

REMEMBER the date
REMEMBER the names

MAY 25 1951

MACLEAN   BURGESS

Remember the faces behind a mystery.

THE HUNT MUST GO ON

by JOHN MATHER

HOW long do you suppose it will be before Donald Maclean and Guy Burgess, the missing diplomats, are tracked down to the activities on which they are engaged—or, if it be the case, to their joint or separate graves?

Here today is the second anniversary of their defection, and despite all the efforts of the Foreign Office, with its maze of ramifications, despite all the sorties by the Special Branch and M.I.5, despite all the concentrated inquiries by the newspapers, all that we appear to know is that Maclean may be alive.

"DAILY EXPRESS"
London, May 25, 1953

RE: GUY BURGESS ET AL
ESPIONAGE

63 JUN 29 1953

DELETED COPY SENT C.B. Mac Donald
BY LETTER JUN 22 1976
PER FOIA REQUEST

OFFICE OF THE LEGAL ATTACHE
AMERICAN EMBASSY
LONDON, ENGLAND

100-374/83

100-374/183
NOT RECORDED
96 JUN 29 1953   28

TODAY two years later

DIPLOMATS: £1,000 REWARD

THE OFFER STILL STANDS

For Gu Burges erratic and shiftless, but a man the Foreign Office judged suitable to be Second Secretary at Washington, has vanished not only from Western eyes but also from the rumours which followed his disappearance.

Maclean, however, has been variously reported seen in Switzerland, then Prague, and then Warsaw. Currency valued at £1,000 was placed in a Swiss bank by, British Intelligence believes, an emissary of Maclean.

And recent international events have pointed to the presence in the Kremlin of just such a propaganda expert as Maclean.

It has been obvious that since the death of Stalin—ignoring all questions of policy—the very methods of the Kremlin have changed. And if you examine the way Russia has conducted herself you may well conclude that she is taking advantage of a Western mind—of a Western mind's knowledge of Western reactions.

For reactions in Britain to Russia's sudden concessions have been precisely what some person or persons in the Kremlin had calculated. Who is advising the Communist sector on propaganda policy?

Pressure

WELL, in Washington it is confidently asserted that Donald Maclean, former head of the American Department in the Foreign Office, is there—pretty close to the Kremlin.

What steps, then, is the British Government now taking to pursue its inquiries into the whereabouts of Maclean and Burgess?

What steps has the Foreign Office taken to ensure that men as close as they were to the heart of Britain's storehouse of secrets can never, some other Friday night, do likewise?

For two years the Daily Express has asked these questions, nay, thundered them. For two years every sort of pressure has been put on the Daily Express with a view to hushing up this scandal.

The Daily Express, however, will not be hushed, as this article bears witness. We, moreover, add today this question:—

May it not be that the unearthing of the full facts about Maclean and Burgess would cause embarrassment and displeasure to (1) certain of their numerous friends, and (2) those class-and-club-conscious people who feel that Maclean and Burgess, despite anything and everything, are superior types who should be protected from the public scrutiny?

A growl

SEE, for a few moments, how the record has run:—

Who, in the first place, told Britain and the world that two British diplomats had vanished? Was it the Foreign Office? Indeed not. It was the Daily Express. And for this public service the reward was an irritated growl from Mr. Herbert Morrison, then his Majesty's Principal Secretary of State for Foreign Affairs.

An M.P. asked him on June 11, 1951, four days after the Daily Express had given the news, and 17 days after the diplomats had gone: "How did this information come to be made public, having regard to the need for keeping it as secret as possible until the Foreign Secretary was in a position to deal with the facts of the case?"

Mr. Morrison replied: "When inquiries were instituted on the Continent it was possible they would leak. We did not at first issue our own announcement for the reason given by the questioner, but we had to do so. One national morning newspaper had some information and had already published a story about it."

'Mania'

SO a calamitous breach in Britain's security precautions was to be hidden and the decamping diplomats given every chance to escape public vigilance—until Mr. Morrison had a chance to "deal with the facts of the case."

Other newspapers were quick to seize the point. The London Star commented in an editorial:—

"This is 'security mania.' If the diplomats have been kidnapped or have voluntarily gone East, then clearly 'security' could not hide the facts from those responsible.

"Why hide them from the people of Britain? Why was it naughty of the Daily Express to print the story?"

The Daily Mail added:—

"Pressure of public opinion, which the newspapers represent, may yet compel the Government to be more forthcoming in the case of the missing diplomats."

Why reward?

WHEN, three weeks later, officialdom could still not deal with the facts of the case because, presumably, it did not possess the facts, the Daily Express took matters further—and offered £1,000 reward for information which would clear up the mystery.

Why did the Daily Express do that? On the ground that it is the duty of a democracy to stay alert and vigilant. On the ground that the public conscience would be uneasy until the final answers were established. On the ground that the security of the Realm might be involved.

The theme was now taken up and, in the Commons, Mr. Morrison declared that security checks were made on members of the Foreign Service on their appointment and, if necessary, from time to time.

Whereupon he was asked whether, on the last check-up, the Foreign Office had been satisfied that Burgess had no Communist affiliations.

What steps has the Foreign Office taken to ensure that men as close as they were to the heart of Britain's storehouse of secrets can never do likewise?

286

Sacked at last

MR. MORRISON replied: "I did not imply that there is a regular and systematic week-by-week check-up of all Foreign Office officials. . . . Indeed, I do not think that the Department deserves such a check-up."

With such complacencies the Socialist Government, in the course of months, went out of office; and in July last Mr. Nutting, Tory Under-Secretary at the Foreign Office, at long last announced that the diplomats had been sacked.

When, however, he was asked to set up a fact-finding commission to inquire into the disappearance of Maclean and Burgess he turned it down with the assurance that "inquiries are continuing."

'Sympathetic'

THOSE latter - day inquiries, pressed on the Government, must have borne fruit; for last October Lord Reading, Joint Under-Secretary with Mr. Nutting, announced in the Lords:—

"Much information about Mr. Maclean has come to light since his disappearance which was not in the possession of the Foreign Office at the time he was appointed head of the American Department in October 1950.

"It is now known, for example, that on more than one occasion before his disappearance Mr. Maclean made remarks suggesting he was a Communist or sympathetic to Communism."

An interview

IT had taken the Foreign Office 17 months to declare itself on associations of the diplomats which the Foreign Office should have known before the men vanished and which the Daily Express had made clear from the start.

And indeed, from the start, the Daily Express inquiries were unceasing. In the course of those inquiries this newspaper obtained an innocuous interview with Mrs. Melinda Maclean, the American-born wife and closest living link of the vanished diplomat.

The interview was based on the not unimportant news, issued by the Press Association, that Mrs. Maclean was leaving England for good. The Daily Telegraph obtained an interview with Mrs. Maclean in similar terms.

But against the Daily Express the furies were unleashed. There were public charges of faking, of invasion of privacy, and there were calls for a curb on this newspaper's unquenchable exuberance. Lady Violet Bonham Carter, a prominent figure in the Liberal Party, persuaded The Times to lend its authority to this propaganda.

In answer to all this came the declaration:—

"The Daily Express does not propose to be deflected from the publication of news because it causes displeasure."

When, therefore, three weeks ago, Mr. David Lawrence, a distinguished political commentator, propounded his certainty in 240 American newspapers that Donald Maclean was in Moscow, the Daily Express published his expert views—and, to foot them, renewed its offer of the £1,000 reward.

Monstrous

AND today the offer still stands. The Daily Express will, relentlessly and remorselessly, pursue its course to aid authority in the search for Maclean and Burgess.

The Daily Express will withstand all pressures when it seeks to serve the public interest. And, make no mistake, it is in the public interest that those absconders should be tracked down — and their defection measured.

That two men rich in the secrets of the Foreign Office should be able to flee these shores and remain unaccountable to British Authority is proof of a monstrous weakness in the security safeguards of the British people.

The weakness must be probed, diagnosed, and remedied.

287

MACLEAN 'GUIDES SOVIET'

Missing diplomat in peace move

—U.S. EXPERT DECLARES

By JOHN MATHER, Express News-Analysis Bureau

A LEADING American political commentator declared yesterday that Donald Maclean, the missing British diplomat, is "undoubtedly" guiding Russia's new peace overtures.

Donald Maclean, who had been Head of the American Department at the Foreign Office, vanished nearly two years ago with Guy Burgess, former second secretary at Washington.

Yesterday's declaration about Maclean was made by Mr. David Lawrence. He is the editor of U.S. News and World Report, and he writes an influential daily political column, which is syndicated to 240 newspapers.

DONALD DUART MACLEAN

DAILY EXPRESS
London 4-28-53

RE: GUY BURGESS, ET AL
ESPIONAGE - R

DELETED COPY SENT C. B. MacDonald
BY LETTER JUN 22 1976
PER FOIA REQUEST

OFFICE OF THE LEGAL ATTACHE
AMERICAN EMBASSY
LONDON, ENGLAND

MAY 1 1953

In his column yesterday, which appeared in such newspapers as the New York Herald Tribune and the Washington Star, he said this :—

"The Soviets play their chess game well. Undoubtedly, they are being guided by Donald Maclean, the British diplomat.

"Maclean, after serving a long time at the British Embassy in Washington, was assigned to take charge of the all - important 'American Desk' in the London Foreign Office through which all confidential cables flowed daily.

"When he disappeared behind the Iron Curtain the then Secretary of State, Mr. Dean Acheson, exclaimed : 'My God, he knew everything !'

"What Maclean knows basically is the weakness and vulnerability of the allied position on the diplomatic side, particularly the situation in Britain where a wedge has been successfully driven between the Washington and London viewpoints."

Atlantic call

From the Daily Express News Analysis Bureau in London I called Mr. Lawrence in Washington, and over the Transatlantic telephone invited him to expand his views.

Mr. Lawrence said : "The publication of President Eisenhower's speech in Pravda—an unusual departure and a clever one—indicates that an Anglo-Saxon mind is in Moscow advising on propaganda.

"That would be someone who knew that the publication of the speech would appeal to Western notions of 'fair play'—notions which Russia has h.therto ignored."

Mr. Lawrence was asked whether he thought any other examples of recent Russian propaganda could be linked with a Westerner's advice.

Sentiment

"Yes," he said, "ever since the Russians have been exchanging prisoners and talking about sending prisoners back, they have realised how sentimental we are about the return of a few people who have been sick and wounded.

"That is another example of how they have suddenly seen our vulnerabilities on the propaganda side."

Mr. Lawrence was asked: "Why do you suspect Donald Maclean at work in Moscow rather than Guy Burgess ?"

He replied : "Maclean was head of the American Desk in the British Foreign Office and would understand exactly how the Western mind reacts.

"He would know more about our diplomatic relations than anyone else.

"Every recent move the Russians have made is the kind of move an Anglo-Saxon would make if he were sitting in Moscow."

Pointers

I then turned to earlier reports which could bear out Mr. Lawrence's view :—

1 Last December came a report that Maclean and Burgess were working in Moscow on an English - language propaganda magazine called News.

2 Then came a report that the diplomats were preparing propaganda leaflets for dropping behind the allied lines in Korea.

3 Mr. Cyril Connolly wrote of Maclean in his book "The Missing Diplomats": "One day towards the end of 1950 Donald invited me to luncheon and talked at length about the war in Korea.

"His argument was that what mattered most in the world was people. The Koreans were people. . . . It was essential at all costs to stop the war and get them established as people again."

£1,000 REWARD
RENEWED
TODAY

DIPLOMATS
£1,000 REWARD

—the Daily Express reward offer, June 30, 1951.

DONALD MACLEAN and Guy Burgess landed from a Channel steamer at St. Malo on May 26, 1951. They took a taxi to Rennes, a town in Brittany—and vanished.

A month later the Daily Express offered £1,000 reward. It was in these terms :—

"The Daily Express offers a reward of £1,000 for information that will establish the whereabouts of the disappearing diplomats Donald Duart Maclean and Guy Francis de Money Burgess.

"This reward will be paid to any person who sends to the Daily Express definite evidence that will lead to the solution of the most puzzling mystery in recent years.

"All such information will be carefully sifted and passed on to the security authorities— M.I.5, Scotland Yard Special Branch, and Foreign Office police—for investigation."

In the light of all the disturbing reports of the activities of the missing diplomats, the Daily Express renews that £1,000 offer today.

289

'Pravda' Is Seen Provin
Reds Play West for Sucker

By DAVID LAWRENCE

WASHINGTON, April 26.—It begins to look as if Moscow is playing the United States and the other nations in the free world for suckers. The tip-off in the Soviet chess game is the publication of the recent speech of President Eisenhower and the significant comment along with it in "Pravda" that Russia, too, has her "claims and ideas of what should be done." Every one of the Eisenhower points was met in the officially inspired Soviet press with the usual Communist rebuttals.

This reflects the plan of the Soviet government to overcome war fears and strengthen a weak internal situation by starting "discussions" which may last two or three years. Meanwhile, the Allies will be influenced by a peace-hungry public opinion to follow a namby-pamby policy of watchful waiting and reduced armament building.

The Soviets are so sure they have the free world in a trap that even while Mr. Eisenhower and the other statesmen call for "deeds, not words," the Communist-supplied armies in the last few days have boldly crossed the boundaries of Laos, an independent kingdom in southeast Asia, thus perpetrating a new aggression before the eyes of the whole world. Moscow guessed right—both Washington and London were too impressed by the "peace maneuvers" to risk any denunciation of what happened in Laos.

Good Chess Players

The Soviets play their chess game well. Undoubtedly they are being guided by Douglas MacLean, the British diplomat, who, after serving a long time at the British Embassy in Washington, then was assigned to take charge of the all-important "American desk" in the London Foreign Office through which all confidential cables flowed daily. When he disappeared behind the Iron Curtain a year and a half ago, Secretary of State Acheson exclaimed, "My God, he knew everything."

What MacLean knows basically is the weakness and vulnerability of the Allied position on the diplomatic side, particularly the situation in Britain where a wedge has been successfully driven between the Washington and London viewpoints, although it has looked lately as if Washington was beginning to succumb to the London concept of peace at any price. No inference of lack of courage need be drawn from

the trend of British diplomatic policy. It is rather an obsession in London that if Asia is written off and any kind of peace is made there, the Allies will be freed to build up their defenses and America will spend more money in Europe.

Story on Montgomery

The story is going around Washington, for instance, that at a private dinner here, given two weeks ago by Gen. Collins, chief of staff of the United States Army, in honor of Viscount Montgomery, the British field marshal—who is deputy military commander of NATO—told the high-ranking guests bluntly that if the American government insisted on carrying the war further in Korea she would find herself alone bearing 100 per cent of the burden; that she could not expect any help from Britain, and that he thought the American people wouldn't go along either. At this, Rep. Dewey Short, Republican, chairman of the House Armed Services Committee, who was at the dinner, is reported to have remarked that he thought he understood somewhat better the feelings of the American people, and since they were today bearing 95 per cent of the burden in Korea, he didn't think they would object to carrying 100 per cent if necessary.

There is no doubt that what Field Marshal Montgomery said privately is no secret in London. Every one there knows that the British government wants the Korean War ended on the principal terms laid down by the Red Chinese, or the Moscow government, as the case may be, because of a belief that this is the way to get more man power and money to strengthen Europe's defenses.

Red Maneuver Seen

Knowing that the government of Great Britain and British public opinion are almost unanimous in opposition to American policy in Korea, the Soviet diplomats are pressing for a general peace conference, where they are confident those differences will be accentuated, or where the U. S. government is expected to capitulate in the face of a united European demand.

So the Russians have everything to gain and nothing to lose by long-drawn-out negotiations. They know, too, that the American-British cry of "deeds, not words," is just rhetoric, because the American and British governments are going to sit down, anyway, with ( ) Con...unists, no matter whe...er any "deeds" are really f...hcoming. Churchill is so e... he is reported to be ready to ...ly to Moscow at a moment's notice.

As for the "deeds," the Soviets will sacrifice a few pawns in their chess game — pieces that are not too important because they will strengthen the other pieces or factors in the game to which they will hold on. Thus, knowing the psychology of the peace-craving free world, Russia's proposal to exchange a few sick and wounded prisoners has already brought a wide demand for peace talks.

A Russian "Deed"

This is what the Russians call a "deed." They may even agree —for a price—to stop the fighting in Korea, knowing well they can frustrate the main objective of the war from the Allied side, which has been to get a "united Korea." This objective has already been discarded by the British, who are willing to agree to a "divided Korea." Also the British are willing, if other terms are met, to admit Red China into the United Nations, whereas Washington is not. This is typical of the opportunities for dissension which the Soviets welcome.

The peace palavers will go on indefinitely, the Soviets will gain valuable time to manufacture more atomic bombs. Moscow will then take the risk of further aggression and will assume that the free world will remain pacifistic. But such aggression will inevitably be met with force when the free world is disillusioned, and then the third world war will come just as surely as the bombardment of Poland came after the appeasement at Munich.

Events are drifting according to historical precedent and that could mean large-scale war within three years, though the exact length of the interval may have to be measured by the time the Allies will give Moscow to build up her machinery and needed raw materials. For already the true purpose of the "peace talks" can be seen clearly—it is to open up East and West trade, which, unfortunately, the British are eager to do. They supplied munitions to Hitler up to a month before he declared war in 1939, and have forgotten already that they furnished—as did America to Japan before 1941—the metals that later helped to kill and maim noncombatants and troops of the free world in World War II.

MacArthur Offers Plan

The alternative to all this was clearly given by Gen. MacArthur in his letter to Sen. Byrd, made public over the week end. It provides a definite, positive policy of resoluteness with an announced threat to use maximum power in Korea unless our terms are met now. But the headlines tell the story of what happened to MacArthur's proposal—the peace-at-any-price sentiment is so strong that sharp denunciation of his suggestions has come from many sides as "rocking the boat" or "throwing a monkey wrench" into the so-called "peace" parleys.

Some day the history books will pick up the MacArthur message of 1953 just as they now pick up the warnings given by Churchill and Eden in the '30s when the Chamberlain government pursued the fatal course of appeasement that encouraged Hitler to risk war. It's odd that as yet Churchill and Eden do not see the peril in today's parallel.

291

THE MISSING DIPLOMATS

by Cyril Connolly

THOSE who become obsessed with a puzzle are not very likely to solve it. Here is one about which I have brooded for a year and would like to unburden myself. Something of what I have put down may cause pain; but that I must risk, because where people are concerned the truth can never be ascertained without painful things being said, and because I feel that what I put down may lead to somebody remembering the fact or phrase which will suddenly bring it all into focus.

If I did not believe (by instinct rather than reason) that the two people about whom I am going to write may well have been victims of some unforeseen calamity, the puzzle would not exist and I should have nothing to say.

I have had access to no secrets. I have not talked to many of the people I should like to. I offer no solution, only a few suggestions, a meditation on human complexity which leads to murky bypaths but which, I hope, will show that no one has any right to jump to unfavourable conclusions about people of whom they know nothing.

A Matter of Choice or Necessity

THE disappearance, towards the end of May last year, of Guy Burgess and Donald Maclean is a mystery which cannot be solved while so many factors remain unknown, and therefore any explanation can be based only on balance of probabilities.

Such solutions fall into two categories, according as they presuppose the disappearance to be a matter of choice or of necessity.

A voluntary flight might be political, as that of Hess to Scotland, or of a private and psychological nature, as when two boys run away from school.

The compelled exit, the forced move, implies escape under duress, the threat being either of private blackmail or of public exposure; or again it might be the result of an imperious recall by a Power which regarded one or both of the two diplomats as in danger or as having become too dangerous.

There remains a possibility that they were sent abroad on a secret mission, and another that they were lured abroad and then kidnapped.

There are simply not enough facts to exclude any of these explanations, nor can we even presume that the behaviour of both Maclean and Burgess is covered by the same explanation. The most striking fact—the suddenness of their disappearance—suggests a panic, but even this suddenness could have been counterfeited. The spontaneous thoroughness of the search would seem to indicate that the Foreign Office first accepted the theory of kidnapping, and so would tend to exclude the notion of a secret mission (unless self-imposed), while a high French police official has maintained that it would have been impossible for the two visitors to France to elude the drag-net spread for them without the "protection" of a political organisation. There are, however, countries where it might be possible for two able-bodied men to obtain work and still escape notice, but they are not so easily reached from the station at Rennes, in Brittany, whence they vanished on May 26, 1951. One must also consider the possibility that they are dead.

As one of the many who knew both, and as one of the few who spoke with Maclean on his last day in England, I should like to approach the subject from a different standpoint. Let us put aside the facts of which we know so little and consider the personalities involved. In so far as one individual can ever understand another, we may find that we have grounds to eliminate some of these explanations and so narrow down the value of X, as we shall name the factor responsible for their joint disappearance.

Looking Back to Childhood

TWO facts distinguish Burgess and Maclean from the so-called "atomic" spies—first, they are not known to have committed any crime, second, they are members of the governing class, of the high bureaucracy, the "they" who rule the "we" to whom refugees like Fuchs and Pontecorvo and humble figures like Nunn May belong. If traitors they be, then they are traitors to themselves. But, as in all cases where people seem to act against their own political interests, we must go back to childhood.

Politics begin in the nursery; no one is born patriotic or unpatriotic, right-wing or left-wing, and it is the child whose craving for love is unsatisfied, whose desire for power is thwarted, or whose innate sense of justice is warped, that eventually may try to become a revolutionary or a dictator. In England we attach spiritual values alone to childhood and adolescence, dismissing political actions of a subversive nature as youthful escapades. But in fact such behaviour in the young is often revealing because it expresses the true meaning of the relationship with the father in its most critical phase.

Guy Burgess lost his father at an early age, and his mother (to whom he is devoted) remarried; Maclean is the child of distinguished Liberal parents; his father, who was then President of the Board of Education, died when he was nineteen.

Burgess was born in 1911.

The Sunday Times
London, Sept. 21, 1952

Re: Donald Duart MacLean, et al. Espionage - R

Maclean in 1913. The one reached Cambridge by way of Eton and Trinity, the other two years later by Gresham's School and Trinity Hall. They knew each other at Cambridge and were both members of the left-wing circle there. But there is no evidence of that oppressive parental authority which drives young men to revolt.

Pre-War Cambridge Marxists

IT was more than ten years since the end of the first world war, and a new generation was growing up which found no outlet in home politics for the adventurous or altruistic impulses of the adolescent. Marxism satisfied both the rebelliousness of youth and its craving for dogma.

The Cambridge Communists substituted a new father or super-ego for the old one, and accepted a new justice and a stricter authority. They felt they had exposed the weaknesses of Liberalism along with their elders' ignorance of economic affairs. To this generation Communism made an intellectual appeal, standing for love, liberty and social justice and for a new approach to life and art. Yet it was connected with a political party, and this party is not inclined to relinquish its hold. "The Comintern," says Arthur Koestler, "carried on a white-slave traffic whose victims were young idealists flirting with violence." The feelings of such young men are described in numerous novels and poems, or in such tracts as Mr. Stephen Spender's "Forward from Liberalism." They involved betrayal of the writers' own country, and the dose of Marxism was seldom lethal.

What were these two young men like? Donald Maclean was sandy-haired, tall, with great latent physical strength, but fat and rather flabby. Meeting him, one was conscious of both amiability and weakness. He did not seem a political animal but resembled the clever helpless youth in a Huxley novel, an outsize Cherubino intent on amorous experience but too shy and clumsy to succeed. The shadow of an august atmosphere lay heavy on him, and he sought refuge on the more impetuous and emancipated fringes of Bloomsbury and Chelsea. Such a young man can be set right by the devotion of an intelligent, older woman, and it was a misfortune that Donald was just not quite able to inspire such attachment; charming, clever and affectionate, he was still too uninformed.

Guy Burgess, though he preferred the company of the able to the artistic, also moved on the edge of the same world. He was of a very different physique, tall - medium in height, with blue eyes, an inquisitive nose, sensual mouth, curly hair and alert fox-terrier expression. He was immensely energetic, a great talker, reader, boaster, walker, who swam like an otter and drank, not like a feckless undergraduate, as Donald was apt to do, but like some Rabelaisian bottle-swiper whose thirst was unquenchable.

Contrasts in Their Characters

THE physical type to which Donald Maclean, despite his puppy fat, belonged was that of the elongated, schizophrenic, sad-countenanced Don Quixote—introverted and diffident, an idealist and a dreamer given to sudden outbursts of aggression; whereas Guy Burgess, despite his intelligence, was a round-faced, golden-pated Sancho Panza, extrovert, exhibitionist, manic, cynical and argumentative, avidly curious, yet sometimes vague and incompetent. With all his toughness, moreover, Guy Burgess wanted intensely to be liked and was indeed likeable, a good conversationalist and an enthusiastic builder-up of his friends. Beneath the "terribilità" of his Marxist analyses one divined the affectionate moral cowardice of the public schoolboy.

An old Etonian, an "Apostle" who had taken a First in History at Cambridge, and was tempted to become a don, he yet seemed an adventurer with a first-class mind, who would always be in the know, a framer of secret policies, a financial wizard already and a future editor, at least, of "The Times." Though he enjoyed a bout of luxury, he was indifferent to appearances and even hostile to his own. Unlike Donald, he concealed his sexual diffidence by over-confidence.

What was common to both Burgess and Maclean at this time was their instability: both were able and ambitious young men of high intelligence and good connections who were somehow parodies of what they set out to be. Nobody could take them quite seriously; they were two characters in a late Russian novel, Laurel and Hardy engaged to play Talleyrand, and the younger Pitt. Burgess, incidentally, was a great reader of fiction; his favourite authors were Mrs. Gaskell and Balzac and, later on, Mr. E. M. Forster. "Lenin had said somewhere that he had learnt more about France from Balzac's novels than from all history-books put together. Accordingly Balzac was the greatest writer of all times." (Koestler.)

Donald was seldom heard to talk politics. Guy never seemed to stop. He was the type of bumptious Marxist who saw himself as Saint-Just, who enjoyed making the flesh of his bourgeois listeners creep by his picture of the justice which history would mete out to them. Grubby, intemperate and promiscuous, he loved to moralise over his friends and satirise their smug class-unconscious behaviour, so reckless of the reckoning in store. But when bedtime came, very late, and it was the moment to put the analyses away, the word "Preposterous" dying on his lips, he would imply a dispensation under which this one house at least, this family, these guests, might be spared the worst consequences, thanks to the protection of their brilliant hunger-marching friend whose position would be so commanding in the happy workers' Utopia.

It was the time when Abyssinia mattered, before the Russian purges had taken place and the especial bitterness of Communist controversy had arisen. There were very few ex-Communists, and the party's claim to represent the extreme left-wing was not disputed. Unlike all other political parties.

THIS IS THE FIRST instalment of Mr. Connolly's personal and intimate study of Guy Burgess and Donald Maclean, the two members of the Foreign Office staff who vanished towards the end of May last year. It will be read with particular interest by those concerned with the peculiar problems arising in an age of ideological conflict which is often projected on the plane of private personality. A second and concluding article will appear next week.

293

ommunism then offered the consolation of a religion.

During the Spanish War I saw
much less of Burgess, who had now
joined the B.B.C. in Bristol. A
horrible thing had happened—he
had become a Fascist! Still sneer-
ing at the bourgeois intellectual, he
now vaunted the intensely modern
realism of the Nazi leaders; his
admiration for economic ruthless-
ness and the short cut to power
had swung him to the opposite
extreme. He claimed to have
attended a Nuremberg Rally.

Maclean, however, a strong sup-
porter of the Spanish Republic,
seemed suddenly to have acquired
backbone, morally and physically.
His appearance greatly improved,
his fat disappeared, and he had
become a personage. In 1935 he
had passed into the Foreign
Office, and from 1938 he was at
the Embassy in Paris.

I remember some arguments
with him. I had felt a great sympathy for the Spanish Anarchists,
with whom he was extremely
severe, as with all the other non-
communist factions, and I detected
in his reproaches the familiar
priggish tone of the Marxist, the
resonance of the "Father Found."
At the same time he could switch
to a magisterial defence of Chamberlain's foreign policy and seemed
able to hold the two self-righteous
points of view simultaneously.

His evenings in Paris were
usually spent in the Left-Bank
cafés with a little group of hard-
working painters and sculptors.
During the daytime he, too,
worked very hard, and it was now
that he began to build up his
reputation in the Foreign Office,
and we must remember that it
grew very high indeed.

Donald had many admirable
Scottish qualities. He was responsible and painstaking, logical and
resolute in argument, judicious
and even-tempered and, I should
imagine, an admirable son and
brother. He had grown much
handsomer, and his tall figure, his
grave long face and noble brow, his
dark suit, black hat and umbrella
were severe and distinguished. One
felt now that he was a rock, that if
one were in trouble he would help
and not just let one down with a
reprimand.

White Hope of the Foreign Office

I REMEMBER, at the beginning
of the war, mentioning to one
of our most famous diplomatic
representatives that Donald was a
friend of mine and receiving a
glance of incredulity. Satisfied
that this indeed was so, he
explained that Maclean was
a white hope, a "puer aureus"
of the Service whose attain-
ments and responsibilities were
well beyond his years. Unlike

Burgess he was without vanity. I
think the simplest distinction
between them is that if you had
given Maclean a letter, he would
have posted it. Burgess would
probably have forgotten it or
opened it and then returned to tell
you what you should have said.

Burgess and a great friend of his
would sometimes stay with a
talented and beautiful woman, a
novelist who, in those days,
resembled an irreducible bastion of
the bourgeoisie entirely surrounded
by Communists, like the Alcazar of
Toledo.

One day Burgess's friend came to
her shaken and yet impressed.
Guy had confided to him that he
was not just a member but a secret
agent of the Communist Party, and
he had then invited him to join in
this work. The friend had refused
with concern; and for her part the
novelist felt that Burgess's
Fascism was suddenly explained:
as a secret agent he must have
been told to investigate the British
Fascists and hoped to pass as one.
Even so, it was impossible to feel
quite certain, for it would be in
keeping with Burgess's neurotic
power-drive that he should pretend
to be an under-cover man.

Years afterwards the novelist
was told that he had spent several
days wrestling with his conscience
at the time of the Soviet-German
pact and had decided to give up
the whole business. This may well
have been true.

Here we have to decide whether
Burgess visited Germany as a
secret Communist, a Nazi sym-
pathiser or as an observer for our
own Intelligence Services, or—at
various levels of his opportunism—
as all three. On one occasion he
took some Boy Scouts over to a
rally at Cologne.

In January, 1939, he left the
B.B.C. and in the autumn of 1940
he was doing confidential work for
the War Office. At this time he was
arrested for being drunk in charge
of a car and acquitted because he
was working fourteen hours a day
and had just
been in an air-
raid.

By January,
1941, he was
once more in the
B.B.C., and there
he remained for
three years in
European propa-
ganda depart-
ments. His posi-
tion became one
that greatly
appealed to him,
involving him
eventually in
liaison work with
highly secret
organisations,
until he was able
to represent the
Foreign Office.
He helped, for instance, to remove
the anti-Russian bias from Poles
whom we were training for
sabotage.

We now see the outline of the
ideal personalities of Burgess and
Maclean. On the unstable founda-
tions of their adolescence they were
erecting the selves whom they
would like to be, the father figures
of their day-dreams, the finished
Imagos. With his black hat and
umbrella, his brief-case under his
arm—O.H.M.S.—Donald is "Sir
Donald Maclean," the Tyrrell, the
Eyre Crowe of the second world
war, the last great Liberal diplo-
matist, terror of the unjust and
hope of the weak. "If it wasn't
for you, Sir Donald," snarled
Ribbentrop, "we might still have
won the peace."

Burgess, of course, is a power
behind the scenes; a brigadier in
mufti, Brigadier Brilliant, D.S.O.,
F.R.S., the famous historian, with
boyish grin and cold blue eyes,
seconded now for special
duties. With long stride and
hunched shoulders, untidy, chain-
smoking, he talks—walks and talks
—while the whole devilish simpli-
city of his plan unfolds and the
men from M.I. this and M.I. that,
S.I.S. and S.O.E., listen dumb-
founded. "My God, Brilliant, I
believe you're right—it could be
done." The Brigadier looked at his
watch and a chilled blue eye fixed
the chief of the Secret Service.
"At this moment, sir," and there
was pack-ice in his voice, "my
chaps are doing it."

Burgess's War-Time Life

IN 1940 Donald Maclean had married in Paris an American girl
as delightful as her name, Melinda
Marling, who bore him two sons.
She brought both sweetness and
understanding into his life. Guy
Burgess, however, as the war went
on, led a more troubled existence.
A new friend whom he had made
was taken prisoner-of-war, and it
was noted that he had become
much more insulting and destructive when he drank—he seemed to
hit on the unforgivable thing to
say to everyone. His mental
sadism, which sometimes led to his
getting knocked out, did not
exclude great kindness to those in
trouble. Above all, he disliked
anyone to get out of his clutches;
he was an affectionate bully
capable of acts of generosity, like a
magnate of the Dark Ages.

At the same time he was drinking and living extravagantly. He
was fond of luxury and display, of
suites at Claridges and fast cars
which he drove abominably. He
belonged to the febrile war-time
café-society of the temporary Civil
Servant, Maclean to the secret
citadel of the permanent.

294

The position of Russia as an ally
made things easier for Communists, who at first were able to
serve their own and their adopted
country without a conflict.
Waverers returned to their allegi-
ance and those who had never
wavered were suddenly respected.
Burgess now had a friend, a foreign
diplomat, whom he considered the
most interesting man he had ever
met and with whom he carried on
a verbal crusade in favour of Communism, each taking a different
line with the potential convert, one
rough, one smooth.

We may distinguish a certain
pattern in Burgess's relationships.
A romantic friendship he liked to
dominate, but his intellectual
admiration was usually kept for
those who were older than himself.
There were also cronies with whom
he preferred to drink and argue.
In June, 1944, he had been trans-
ferred to the News Department of
the Foreign Office, in 1946 to the
office of the Minister of State, Mr.
Hector McNeil, in 1947 to B branch
Foreign Office, and in 1948 to the
Far-Eastern Department of the
Foreign Office.
In 1944, the year that Guy Burgess went from the B.B.C. to the
Foreign Office Donald Maclean was
posted to Washington as acting First Secretary. On his
return in 1948 he gave a
"inner-party" to his friends. It
was a delightful evening. he had
become a good host, his charm was
based not on vanity but on
sincerity, and he would discuss
foreign affairs as a student, not
an expert. He enjoyed the magazine that I then edited, which was
a blue rag to Burgess, a weak injec-
tion of culture into a society
already dead
On his return from Washington
he was appointed Counsellor in
Cairo. "In Donald Maclean I see a
courage and a love of justice; I see a
soul that could not be deflected
from the straight course; and I see
in it that deep affection for his
friends which he always mani-
fested." The words of Stanley
Baldwin about the father seemed to
be coming true of the son. A
Counsellor at thirty-five, he seemed
in a fair way to equal his parent's
distinction.

A Breakdown in Cairo

IN 1950 word began to reach us
that all was not so well. It was
said that Donald, whose high
Liberal principles had received full
scope in enlightened Washington,
had been so disheartened by the
poverty and corruption of the
Middle East that he had had some
kind of breakdown. It seems that
he adopted a theory that sufficient
alcohol could release in one a
second personality which, though
it might simulate the destructive
element, worked only good by help-
ing people to acknowledge the truth
about themselves and reveal their
latent affinities. Donald entered
into the spirit of the investigation
and took as his *alter ego* the name
of "Gordon" from an export gin
with a tusky wild boar on the label.

When night fell his new self took
possession. He stampeded one or
two parties, but got into more
serious trouble when, in the company of a friend, he broke into the
first apartment to hand in a block
of flats and sharpened his tusks on
the furniture.

Then on a boating trip on the
Nile, with some twenty people in
the party, he seized a rifle from an
officious sentry and began to imperil
the safety of those nearest him by
swinging it wildly. A Secretary at
the Embassy intervened, and in the
scuffle received a broken leg. The
two men returned home on sick
leave, while Mrs. Maclean who was
on the boating trip, went to Spain
for a rest with her two sons.

What was the nature of Donald's
outburst? It was not just overwork, but over-strain; the effort of
being "Sir Donald," the whole
paraphernalia of "O.H.M.S.," had
been too much for him and he had
reverted to his adolescence, or to
his ideal of Paris days, the free and
solitary young sculptor working all
night in his attic. The return of
the repressed is familiar to psycho-
analysts, and there was also now a
brief return to his early sexual
ambivalence. "Gordon" had given
"Sir Donald" the sack. The
enraged junior partner would no
longer put up with him.

Six Months' Leave for Maclean

BACK in London he had six
months' leave to get well and to
make up his mind about the future.
He was still drinking and was now
undergoing treatment from a
woman psycho-analyst. His appearance was frightening; he had lost
his serenity, his hands would
tremble, his face was usually a
livid yellow and he looked as if he
had spent the night sitting up in
a tunnel. Though he remained
detached and amiable as ever, it
was clear that he was miserable
and in a very bad way. In conversation a kind of shutter would
fall as if he had returned to
some basic and incommunicable
anxiety.

Some of his friends urged him to
resign, pointing out that since he
disliked the life and disagreed with
the policy he could not go back
without it all happening again.
Others assured him that he would
soon be well enough to return to
work, which would prove the best
thing for himself and his family.
The Foreign Office had to weigh
his years of hard work against
the outburst, which they put down
to the strain of long hours and
formal social duties in Cairo and
Washington. His reputation for a
penetrating mind, sound judgment
and quiet industry turned the scale.
The psychiatrist's reports became
more encouraging, and by the
autumn the decision was taken. On
November 6, after a particularly
heavy night, Donald went back to
the Foreign Office as head of the
American Division (a position less
onerous than it sounds and which
involved no social duties), and he
bought a house near Westerham
for his wife and children, to which
he hoped to return almost every
evening, avoiding the temptations
of the city.

[To be continued]

295

THE MISSING
by Cyril Connolly
DIPLOMATS—II

Last week Mr. Connolly depicted the early lives of Guy Burgess and Donald Maclean. In 1935 Maclean passed into the Foreign Office, where his reputation soon mounted. Burgess went from the B.B.C. to the Foreign Office in 1944, and was in the Far-Eastern Department in 1948.

In 1944 Maclean was posted to Washington as acting First Secretary, and on his return four years later was appointed Counsellor in Cairo. But in Cairo came a breakdown. On November 6, 1950, after six months' leave, he went back to the Foreign Office as head of the American Division.

ONE day towards the end of 1950 Donald Maclean invited me to luncheon at his club and talked at length about the war in Korea. His argument was that what mattered most in the world was people. The Koreans were people, but in the stage which the war had reached both sides had entirely forgotten this, and were exploiting them for their own prestige. It was essential to stop the war at all costs and get them established as people again.

This was not the orthodox Communist view, according to which only the North Koreans were "people" and the South Koreans (as Burgess maintained) had really started the war. Maclean went on to suggest that all colonial possessions in the Far East were morally untenable, and when I pleaded that we should be allowed to keep Hongkong and Malaya for their dollar-earning capacities he said that that was precisely the reason why we should give them up, as only then could we prove ourselves in earnest and lay the basis of future good relations.

Back at the Foreign Office

WE talked for a little about how he felt at being back at work and "Sir Donald" again, and he told me how fond he was of his colleagues, how secure and womb-like the Foreign Office seemed, and how well he had been treated. I mentioned that I had at one time been intended for the Diplomatic Service and that I had always regarded it since with some of the wistfulness which he felt for literature. We left rather late and he merged on the steps into a little pin-striped shoal of hurrying officials, who welcomed him affectionately.

One evening at the end of that winter a friend came round for a drink. He said that he was in a difficulty: he had been up very late with Donald the night before, and Donald had said to him, "What would you do if I told you I was a Communist agent?"

"I don't know."

"Well, wouldn't you report me?"

"I don't know. Who to?"

"Well, I am. Go on, report me."

His friend had woken up with a confused feeling that something unpleasant lay before him. It was an absurd situation, for it was impossible to be sure that Donald was serious. My friend knew him so well that he could not believe it was true. The whole incident seemed preposterous in the light of day.

Burgess Recalled from Washington

IN August, 1950, Guy Burgess had been posted to the Washington Embassy as Second Secretary; he had last visited Washington in 1942. By the early spring of 1951 things were not going so well for him. The telegrams which he drafted were often rejected as being biased, there seemed nothing for him to do, he was not popular with his colleagues, he was drinking heavily again, and on one day, February 28, he was stopped three times for speeding, which led to an official complaint. Then he gave a lift to a young man and let him take the wheel. There was an accident, and it turned out that the young man had no driving licence. Burgess pleaded diplomatic immunity. At about the same time an English visitor to the Embassy reported him for anti-British talk. He was recalled from Washington as "generally unsuitable" and arrived home in the Queen Mary on May 4.

A few days later I ran into him in the street. He came up with his usual shaggy, snarling-playful manner and said he was just back from America.

"Where were you?"

"Washington."

"What was it like?"

"Absolutely frightful."

"Why?"

"Because of McCarthy." I

"Senator McCarthy," said Burgess. "Terrible atmosphere. All these purges."

He seemed very well and almost jaunty, obviously pleased to be back even if he went around saying he was convinced that America had gone mad and was determined on war.

During the winter Donald Maclean had made a great effort to fit into his new existence as a commuter. Mrs. Maclean was expecting another child, and Donald conscientiously refused to go to cocktail parties in order not to miss his evening train to Kent. By May, however, he seemed to be more about London of an evening, and it would be interesting if we could discover if there was any sudden increase in these outings after the return of Guy Burgess. On one occasion in April, after some feint attacks, he knocked down one of his greatest friends for taking the side of Whittaker Chambers in the Hiss case. Chambers, according to Donald, was a double-faced exhibitionist too revolting to be defended by anyone.

Donald's drinking followed an established routine. The charming and amiable self was gradually left behind, and the hand which patted his friend on the back became a flail. A change would come into his voice like the roll of drums for the cabaret. It took the form of an outburst of indignation, often directed against himself, in which the embittered idealist would abandon all compromise and castigate all forms of humbug and pretence. As the last train left for Sevenoaks from faraway Charing Cross he would wave a large hand, in some bar, to his companions. "Well, anyhow, you're all right. And you are all right." The elected smiled happily, but doubt was spreading like a frown on Caligula. "Wait—I'm not sure. Perhaps you aren't all right. After all, you said this and this. In fact, you're very wrong. You won't do at all. (*Biff*). And as for you—you're the worst of the lot, but I suppose I must forgive you." (*Bash.*)

Unexpected Visit from Maclean

AFTER a dinner-party on May 15 six of us came back to my house: it was divided into two, and Donald occasionally spent the night in the other flat. Past midnight there was a battering on the door and I let him in, sober-drunk, the first time I had seen him in this legendary condition. He began to wander round the room, blinking at the guests as he divided the sheep from the goats, and then went out to lie down to sleep in the hall, stretched out on the stone floor under his overcoat like some figure from a shelter sketch-book. The departing guests had to make their way over him, and I noticed that, although in apparent coma, he would raise his long stiff leg like a drawbridge when one of the goats was trying to pass. I put him to bed in his absent friend's flat and gave him an Alka-Seltzer breakfast in the morning.

On May 25, the day when Burgess and Maclean left England, I arranged to greet some friends in Schmidt's before lunching down the street at the Etoile. We met in the road. Donald was with them, looking rather creased and yellow, casual but diffident. We all stood on the pavement. I said to him, "You're Cyril Connolly, aren't you? —I'm Sir Donald Maclean"; this reference to our conversation at his club was intended to efface our last meeting. He seemed calm and genial, and went off gaily to continue the luncheon with his friends, who were to rejoin me for coffee.

At luncheon, they told me when they came back, he had been mellow and confidential; he had talked about himself, about how much better he felt, how he didn't have to visit his psycho-analyst so often, and how he was determined to take a hold on himself lest he got into any trouble which might bring disgrace upon his children. That day was his birthday. The luncheon was his treat, and the week after he was getting some compassionate leave, for his wife would be going to hospital for the baby; he asked if he could come down and visit my friends for some part of the time. They had been very kind to him when he was ill, and he was now in effect making them a favourable report.

After spending the afternoon in his office he went off to Charing Cross and caught his usual train to Sevenoaks. That evening Burgess arrived at Donald's house at Tatsfield—he had driven down in a hired car—and was introduced to Mrs. Maclean as "Ronald Styles." Burgess had engaged the car by telephone at about two o'clock and then gone round, paid the deposit, and undergone a brief driving test. At 5.30 he had received a long telephone call at his flat.

After a quiet and rather sober dinner Donald and "Ronald" walked in the garden. Donald then said that they had to go to see a friend who lived nearby and that he might have to stay away for the night. He promised that he would return on the morrow and took only his briefcase with him when he left.

Midnight Arrival at Southampton

THE pair got into the hired car and drove to Southampton just in time to reach the cross-Channel vessel Falaise, which left at midnight on a special week-end cruise to Saint Malo and back by the Channel Islands, returning early on Monday morning. "What about the car?" yelled a port garage attendant. Burgess cried: "Back on Monday."

He had booked the two-berth cabin at Victoria on the Wednesday in his own name, and on that day had invited a young American, whom he introduced to various people as "Miller" and whom he had met on the Queen Mary, when returning from Washington, to accompany him. But Burgess let him down at the last moment. Burgess seems to have had the idea of a long holiday in France in his mind, but that was unconnected with the week-end jaunt. For this Friday evening he had an important dinner engagement which he never cancelled.

At Saint Malo, where the boat arrived at 10 a.m., the two stayed on board, breakfasting and drinking beer till the others had left. Then at eleven they, too, went ashore, leaving behind Burgess's two suitcases. At the station, which the Paris express had just left (they would have had plenty of time to catch it) they took a taxi to Rennes, the junction some fifty miles away. They did not speak on the way. They gave no tip to the driver on the fare of 4,500 francs and they arrived at Rennes station in time to catch the express again. They were not noticed on the train, which reached Paris, via Le Mans, between five and six. From that moment they have vanished.

WHEN Burgess had tickets on the Wed said the other name fo would probably be Mill Thursday night he seem an agitated state "look friend who was going He seems to have spen Friday with Miller, fe from the Green Park H morning and lunching At two o'clock he rin his club for the hired the garage with Miller car near his New Bond and goes shopping, buy mackintosh (he had a tosh), a fibre suitcase many nylon shirts wh fit him.

At 5.25 he left M hotel, saying "See yo He then went back received the telephon packed into two suitc brief-case four suits. blue jeans, socks, ha and his gaudy collecti an extensive wardrob nights at sea. At seve last drink at his club. evening the American flat to know why he h fetshed.

Maclean's day was quite inactive. Burgess Maclean the patient, a nothing to show that tended going anywhe was driven off from h Burgess. His birthda lasted from 12.30 unti — champagne and Wheeler's, then some food at Schmidt's; he till 5.30 and he went usual train. But it n the telephone call wh received at 5.30 was so SOS from Maclean.

During May Burgess worries, but he had b an important job on a and he was going out t clinch this on the day

297

thought he had said MacArthur, and asked what he had to do with it.

"Senator McCarthy," said Burgess. "Terrible atmosphere. All these purges."

He seemed very well and almost jaunty, obviously pleased to be back even if he went around saying he was convinced that America had gone mad and was determined on war.

During the winter Donald Maclean had made a great effort to fit into his new existence as a commuter. Mrs. Maclean was expecting another child, and Donald conscientiously refused to go to cocktail parties in order not to miss his evening train to Kent. By May, however, he seemed to be more about London of an evening, and it would be interesting if we could discover if there was any sudden increase in these outings after the return of Guy Burgess. On one occasion in April, after some feint attacks, he knocked down one of his greatest friends for taking the side of Whittaker Chambers in the Hiss case. Chambers, according to Donald, was a double-faced exhibitionist too revolting to be defended by anyone.

Donald's drinking followed an established routine. The charming and amiable self was gradually left behind, and the hand which patted his friend on the back became a flail. A change would come into his voice like the roll of drums for the cabaret. It took the form of an outburst of indignation, often directed against himself, in which the embittered idealist would abandon all compromise and castigate all forms of humbug and pretence. As the last train left for Sevenoaks from faraway Charing Cross he would wave a large hand, in some bar, to his companions. "Well, anyhow, you're all right. And you are all right." The elected smiled happily, but doubt was spreading like a frown on Caligula. "Wait—I'm not sure. Perhaps you aren't all right. After all, you said this and this. In fact, you're very wrong. You won't do at all. (Biff.) And as for you—you're the worst of the lot, but I suppose I must forgive you." (Bash.)

Unexpected Visit from Maclean

AFTER a dinner-party on May 15 six of us came back to my house: it was divided into two, and Donald occasionally spent the night in the other flat. Past midnight there was a battering on the door and I let him in, sober-drunk, the first time I had seen him in this legendary condition. He began to wander round the room, blinking at the guests as he divided the sheep from the goats, and then went out to lie down to sleep in the hall, stretched out on the stone floor under his overcoat like some figure from a shelter sketch-book. The departing guests had to make their way over him, and I noticed that, although in apparent coma, he would raise his long stiff leg like a drawbridge when one of the goats was trying to pass. I put him to bed in his absent friend's flat and gave him an Alka-Seltzer breakfast in the morning.

On May 25, the day when Burgess and Maclean left England, I arranged to greet some friends in Schmidt's before lunching down the street at the Étoile. We met in the road. Donald was with them, looking rather creased and yellow, casual but diffident. We all stood on the pavement. I said to him, "You're Cyril Connolly, aren't you? —I'm Sir Donald Maclean"; this reference to our conversation at his club was intended to efface our last meeting. He seemed calm and genial, and went off gaily to continue the luncheon with his friends, who were to rejoin me for coffee.

At luncheon, they told me when they came back, he had been mellow and confidential; he had talked about himself, about how much better he felt, how he didn't have to visit his psycho-analyst so often, and how he was determined to take a hold on himself lest he got into any trouble which might bring disgrace upon his children.

That day was his birthday. The luncheon was his treat, and the week after he was getting some compassionate leave, for his wife would be going to hospital for the baby; he asked if he could come down and visit my friends for some part of the time. They had been very kind to him when he was ill, and he was now in effect making them a favourable report.

After spending the afternoon in his office he went off to Charing Cross and caught his usual train to Sevenoaks. That evening Burgess arrived at Donald's house at Tatsfield—he had driven down in a hired car—and was introduced to Mrs. Maclean as "Ronald Styles." Burgess had engaged the car by telephone at about two o'clock and then gone round, paid the deposit, and undergone a brief driving test. At 5.30 he had received a long telephone call at his flat.

After a quiet and rather sober dinner Donald and "Ronald" walked in the garden. Donald then said that they had to go to see a friend who lived nearby and that he might have to stay away for the night. He promised that he would return on the morrow and took only his briefcase with him when he left.

Midnight Arrival at Southampton

THE pair got into the hired car and drove to Southampton just in time to reach the cross-Channel vessel Falaise, which left at midnight on a special week-end cruise to Saint Malo and back by the Channel Islands, returning early on Monday morning. "What about the car?" yelled a port garage attendant. Burgess cried: "Back on Monday."

He had booked the two-berth cabin at Victoria on the Wednesday in his own name, and on that day had invited a young American, whom he introduced to various people as "Miller" and whom he had met on the Queen Mary, when returning from Washington, to accompany him. But Burgess let him down at the last moment. Burgess seems to have had the idea of a long holiday in France in his mind, but that was unconnected with the week-end jaunt. For this Friday evening he had an important dinner engagement which he never cancelled.

At Saint Malo, where the boat arrived at 10 a.m., the two stayed on board, breakfasting and drinking beer till the others had left. Then at eleven they, too, went ashore, leaving behind Burgess's two suitcases. At the station, which the Paris express had just left (they would have had plenty of time to catch it) they took a taxi to Rennes, the junction some fifty miles away. They did not speak on the way. They gave no tip to the driver on the fare of 4,500 francs and they arrived at Rennes station in time to catch the express again. They were not noticed on the train, which reached Paris, via Le Mans, between five and six. From that moment they have vanished.

Preparations for a Journey

WHEN Burgess had booked the tickets on the Wednesday he said the other name for the cabin would probably be Miller; and on Thursday night he seemed to be in an agitated state "looking for the friend who was going with him. He seems to have spent much of Friday with Miller, fetching him from the Green Park Hotel in the morning and lunching with him. At two o'clock he rings up from his club for the hired car, visits the garage with Miller, parks the car near his New Bond Street flat and goes shopping, buying a white mackintosh (he had no mackintosh), a fibre suitcase and a good many nylon shirts which did not fit him.

At 5.25 he left Miller at his hotel, saying "See you at 7.30." He then went back to his flat, received the telephone call, and packed into two suitcases and a brief-case four suits, his shirts, blue jeans, socks, handkerchiefs and his gaudy collection of ties—an extensive wardrobe for two nights at sea. At seven he had a last drink at his club. Later that evening the American rang up the flat to know why he had not been fetched.

Maclean's day was apparently quite inactive. Burgess is the agent, Maclean the patient, and there is nothing to show that Donald intended going anywhere until he was driven off from his house by Burgess. His birthday luncheon lasted from 12.30 until after 2.30 — champagne and oysters at Wheeler's, then some more solid food at Schmidt's; he was at work till 5.30 and he went home by his usual train. But it may be that the telephone call which Burgess received at 5.30 was some kind of SOS from Maclean.

During May Burgess had had his worries, but he had been offered an important job on a newspaper and he was going out to dinner to clinch this on the day he vanished.

when he had confided in a friend that at last he would be able to settle down to his great task, the addition of a final volume to Lady Gwendolen Cecil's biography of the Tory Prime Minister, Lord Salisbury, which he thought the best biography in English.

On June 7, as the hue and cry began in the Press, three telegrams arrived: one from Guy Burgess to his mother in which he said he was embarking on a long Mediterranean holiday; and two from Maclean, to his mother and his wife. To Lady Maclean he sent a brief message which he signed with a childhood name, to his wife he wrote: "Had to leave unexpectedly, terribly sorry. Am quite well now. Don't worry, darling. I love you. Please don't stop loving me. Donald." All three sound plausible but somehow unreal, unless they were meant to be delivered at least a week before.

Having acquired a little more background, let us examine some of the theories with which we began. It will be noticed even now how very few facts we have. We suspect that Burgess and Maclean were Communists at Cambridge. we do not know even if they ever met after Cambridge. Both were neurotic personalities with schizophrenic characteristics. In recent posts both had behaved so recklessly that they had to be sent home, both drank too much and then became violent and abusive, both might be described as abnormal, both allegedly made confessions (many years apart) of being Communist agents, and both were notorious among their colleagues for their anti-British arguments and were bitter against authoritarianism and imperialism. Both had risen fast under wartime conditions and had yet maintained an undergraduate-like informality in their appearance and habits and in the general bed-sitting room casualness of their way of life. Both had two enemies, adolescence and alcohol, and when they vanished each was thought by his friends to have led the other astray.

Association that was Kept Secret

THEY had everything in common, in fact, except each other; they were like two similar triangles suddenly superimposed. When Donald met this liberator of irresponsibilities, when Don Quixote found his Sancho Panza, there was bound to be a combustion.

Then how was their association kept secret? I think myself that they must have renewed the Cambridge friendship in the summer of 1950, during Maclean's convalescence, and that Burgess was part of what Maclean called his "ash-can life," of which he was ashamed and trying to cure himself. Hence the secrecy. Were they Communist agents? Surely the first duty of a secret agent is to escape detection, express conventional views and rise in his career. The more Communism they talked the less likely they were to be agents. And Burgess talked a great deal.

Recklessness or Deception?

COULD this have been recklessness or a subtle double bluff? Both are just possible. Maclean, however, in the fifteen years in which I had come across him, remained always devoted to the nonconformist but essentially non-political little group of writers and painters whom he had known in London and Paris. They were his home.

Nor did Burgess ever appear at all calculating. "Guy would help anybody in distress. He would make a split-second decision and carry it out no matter what the consequences. He would certainly not do anything to injure his country."

Like most people who feel they have been starved of love, Burgess and Maclean desired to raise the emotional temperature around them to something higher than in the world outside, and found in drink a consolation. If we believe that emotional maladjustment was the key to their personalities, it is hard to see how they could possess the control to serve a foreign country coolly and ruthlessly for twenty years and yet work all the time in executive capacities for their own.

I think that Burgess was a Marxist in his mental processes and an anti-Marxist individualist in his personality. Maclean, it may be, had something on his conscience, which, however, was a particularly tender one; possibly, above all, he had a fear about his mental condition.

So many explanations of their

disappearance have been put forward that it is best to deal with a few of them like chess-openings. Let us first take one based on the theory of a voluntary escape.

1. NON-POLITICAL. *The two disappeared on an alcoholic fugue, to wander about like Verlaine and Rimbaud and to start a new life together.*

This fits in with Donald's character. He is said to have disappeared once from a party for a few days in Switzerland and been found living quietly in the next village. Again, he once remarked to a friend that he wished he could start a new life as a docker in the East End, but that ration books and identity cards now made it impossible. Burgess also had a reputation for disappearing, but there would be much less reason for him to give up the kind of existence to which he was addicted. Neither could have lasting attraction for the other, for the force which united them would also drive them apart, and the wanderers would certainly have been heard of again, for where they were in company incidents would be bound to arise; and the element of anti-social aggression in such a flight would have caused them to leave some kind of statement.

A Twitch upon the Thread

2. (a) THEORIES WHICH IMPLY A FORCED MOVE. "*A twitch upon the thread.*" The argument is that Burgess and Maclean were both Communist agents, Maclean (or both) was growing indiscreet and unreliable, and that they were recalled before one (or both) could give away others who were more secret and more important; that they were immediately imprisoned or liquidated and may have got no farther than an uncertain address in Paris. If they had refused to go, they would have been exposed to the British and brought disgrace on their families. Even so, it is doubtful if experienced diplomats aged 38 and 40 would sign their own death-warrants without a murmur and depart without a farewell.

(b) *They both (or Maclean alone) had given information to the Russians at some time, perhaps on one occasion only, and this was preying on Donald's conscience.* If the information was given in Washington, it might have been valuable, and the leak would have taken a long time to trace. Burgess might have had wind in Washington of this investigation and even got himself sent home through his erratic behaviour in order to warn Maclean on his return. Burgess might perhaps at one time have been a kind of private commissar to Maclean. After his carefree luncheon, then, on that last Friday, Maclean was somehow tipped off that exposure was imminent. At 5.30 he telephones to his contact Burgess who says "Leave it all to me."

The Making of a Myth

THIS theory bristles with difficulties, but it does at least explain the sudden departure. And yet, like all who knew him, I am convinced that Donald was not an active Communist. He had a morbid inclination to suicide, and he would say that only his love for his children kept him from it. This love was the one emotion which he felt without ambivalence, and he would not have taken any drastic step unless he had been convinced that it was for the best as far as their happiness was concerned.

Perhaps Burgess and Maclean are at last integrated. But, as Maclean said, what matters most is people, and that is what makes his case essentially tragic. Guy Burgess always enjoyed being himself, and for a while he lived his own dream, a realistic example of the "new type of diplomat" who is always demanded in wartime. But Donald Maclean, were it not for his lack of balance and emotional security, had the qualities of a great public servant. Yet with all his admiration for people, he betrayed those who loved him, humiliated those who trusted him, and discredited those who thought like him. . . . But once again we are condemning them unheard.

Meanwhile a myth is slowly transfiguring them. At first they were seen in Montmartre and Montparnasse, in Brussels and Bayonne, on the high pass to Andorra, in a bar in Cannes and, with brimming glasses, in a garden-restaurant of Prague.

This year they have been heard of playing chess in the Lubianka prison and running an import-export business in Prague; and Guy Burgess as visiting Browning's villa ("What's become of Waring?") north-east of Venice. And so for many years they will be seen until the mystery is solved. If it ever is, haunting the Old World's pleasure-traps about the season of their disappearance, bringing with them strawberries and hot weather and escapist leanings: a portent of the middle summer's spring.

THIS IS THE CONCLUDING *instalment of Mr. Connolly's personal and intimate study of Guy Burgess and Donald Maclean, the two members of the Foreign Office Staff who vanished on May 26, 1951. Their crucial last day in England—Maclean's birthday—is closely examined.*

300

New home for Mrs Maclean

ZURICH, Tuesday.—Mrs. Melinda Maclean, wife of the missing diplomat, intends to live with her mother in Geneva. Mrs. Maclean told authorities she wanted to make Geneva her permanent home, if she found she could live there unmolested.—*D.M. Reporter*

DAILY MAIL
London, England
October 22, 1952

RE: DONALD STUART BURGESS,
ET AL. ESPIONAGE - R

53 NOV 7 1952

OFFICE OF THE LEGAL ATTACHE
AMERICAN EMBASSY
LONDON, ENGLAND

100-374

100-324189-A

NOT RECORDED
9S NOV 3 1952

301

BRITISH SEE PRANK IN 'RED' RECORDING

Foreign Office Says Diplomat Mimicking Churchill Made Platter Ascribed to Another

Special to The New York Times.

LONDON, Oct. 29—The recording of a statement that Lord Elton ascribed to Donald D. Mac-Lean, in which the former Foreign Office official was supposed to have set forth his political views, actually was made by Guy Francis de Moncy Burgess, another British diplomat, who disappeared with Mr. MacLean, the Foreign Office disclosed today.

The Foreign Office spokesman dismissed the matter as of little importance, saying that the recording Lord Elton said had been made in the home of a friend of a member of the House of Lords in the United States, was made in a prankish mood on a night in May 1951 before Mr. Burgess left Washington. A good mimic, Mr. Burgess gave so good an imitation of Prime Minister Churchill that his host insisted on recording the monologue, other sources said.

At the Foreign Office it was said that the recording made no reference to Mr. MacLean or to communism.

Lord Elton said in the House of Lords yesterday that he understood that Mr. MacLean had made a recording in which he had declared himself to be not merely a Communist "but a proselytizing Communist."

He said the recording was in the possession of the Federal Bureau of Investigation, and he implied that the Foreign Office should have known about it prior to the flight of the two diplomats a year ago last May.

Anthony Eden, Foreign Secretary, referred to the Burgess recording at question time in the House of Commons. He said that while there was no record that Mr. MacLean had made a recording Mr. Burgess had made one at a private party. Then the Foreign Secretary added:

"I have not had it played over to me, but I understand it does not contain any profession of Communist views but is for the most part a comic imitation in some cases of a quite well-known public figure."

Both sides of the House shouted to Mr. Eden to name the public figure, but he did not do so.

Elsewhere it was learned that Mr. Burgess was well known for his skillful mimicry of Mr. Churchill. Before World War II, the story goes, Mr. Burgess, then working for the British Broadcasting Company, recorded Mr. Churchill's caustic comments on Munich for the broadcasting corporation.

The recording was not used, but Mr. Burgess kept the record and by long practice became so proficient in imitating the Prime Minister's style that listeners could hardly distinguish between the authentic record and the Burgess imitation, according to the informants.

MISSING BRITISH AID IS CALLED ADMITTED RED

Peer Cites FBI In MacLean Case

LONDON, Oct. 28 (AP)—Donald MacLean, the British diplomat who vanished in mid-1951, suggested "on more than one occasion" that he was a Communist while working for the foreign office, a government spokesman disclosed today.

Lord Reading, parliamentary undersecretary of foreign affairs, told the house of lords questioners, however, that MacLean was not known as a Red sympathizer at the time of his appointment.

MacLean was head of the American department of the foreign office for nine months before he disappeared, possibly behind the Iron Curtain.

Lord Elton told the undersecretary that the American Federal Bureau of Investigation has a recording said to have been made in New York by MacLean in which he "openly declared himself a Communisit.

The FBI, Elton claimed, has had that record in its poossession "for a good many years."

MacLean and a second foreign office colleague, Guy Burgess, disappeared June 7, 1951. Agents traced them as far as France, but then lost all track of them.

100-374183-A
RECORDED
OCT 31 1952

100-374183

Times-Herald _____

Dated *Oct. 29/95*

78 NOV 3 1952

303

LOST BRITON IS SAID TO ADMIT RED TIES

Lords Hear Missing Diplomat's Recording of the Statement Is in Hands of F. B. I.

Special to The New York Times.

LONDON, Oct. 28—Lord Elton declared in the House of Lords today that the United States Federal Bureau of Investigation had in its possession a recording of a statement by Donald D. MacLean, one of two missing Foreign Office diplomats, that he was not only a Communist, but "a proselytizing Communist."

Mr. MacLean, former head of the American section of the Foreign Office disappeared a year ago last May with his friend, Guy Francis de Moncy Burgess, another Foreign Office official. They are believed to be behind the Iron Curtain.

According to Lord Elton, the recording of which he spoke was made by Mr. MacLean in New York in the apartment of a friend of the House of Lords long before Mr. MacLean's disappearance. Lord Elton said he understood that the recording was in the possession of the F. B. I. and said it should not have been impossible for responsible British officials to discover its existence.

Lord Stansgate objected to the suggestion that Britain should "invite the American F. B. I. to assist us in finding out the records of our own public servants."

The Marquess of Reading, Joint Under-Secretary for Foreign Affairs, disclaimed knowledge of the recording to which Lord Elton referred, but agreed that much more was known about Mr. MacLean's drinking habits and political convictions now than before he disappeared. There was no reason to suspect him, Lord Reading said, although he had suffered a breakdown from overdrinking in Cairo and on on occasion had broken a colleague's leg in a fight.

Special to The New York Times.

WASHINGTON, Oct. 28—The Federal Bureau of Investigation refused today to comment on a statement by Lord Elton that Mr. MacLean had admitted that he was a "proselytizing Communist." The F. B. I. has maintained silence regarding its part in the investigation since Mr. MacLean and Mr. Burgess disappeared in June 1951.

MacLean, Missing Diplomat, Had Red Leanings, British Foreign Office Says

By Reuters

London, Oct. 28—The Foreign Office acknowledged for the first time today that Donald MacLean, missing British diplomat, had indicated Communist leanings.

The sensational disappearance of MacLean and his Foreign Office friend, Guy Burgess, 18 months ago gave rise to a flood of rumors that they had fled to Eastern Europe.

Facing a barrage of questions today in the House of Lords, Foreign Undersecretary Lord Reading said: "It is now known that on more than one occasion before his disappearance Mr. MacLean made remarks suggesting he was a Communist or sympathetic to communism."

He also disclosed that MacLean, 38, was prone to violence after drinking and once had broken a colleague's leg.

"It will be realized," Reading said, "that much information about Mr. MacLean has come to light since his disappearance which was not in the possession of the Foreign Office at the time he was appointed head of the American department in October, 1950."

He said "most of the more important questions" in Anglo-American relations were not handled by MacLean's office.

The questions in the House of Lords arose from a series of articles in the Sunday Times, an austerely Conservative newspaper, summing up the mystery of the missing diplomats.

Lord Elton, an independent peer, asked if the government's attention had been drawn to the articles, which alleged MacLean openly had declared himself a Communist and had been drinking heavily.

FBI Has Recording

The articles also called Burgess "a Marxist in his mental processes." Burgess, 40, was a former second secretary at the British Embassy in Washington. Both missing diplomats were emotional, the articles said.

Elton said the American FBI has a recording of a speech made by MacLean during a visit to a private party in New York in which he openly declared himself a "proselytizing Communist.

"We cannot have people listening and taking down notes at every private party which a member of the Foreign Office attends," Reading replied. He added he had no information about the FBI recording.

RS

Maclean And Burgess Seen In Berlin

—Says Deputy Premier Of East Germany

THE East German Deputy Premier said at a luncheon in Bonn yesterday that Donald Maclean and Guy Burgess, the missing British diplomats, had been seen recently in the United States sector of Berlin.

Without elaborating, Herr Nuschke said the case of Burgess and Maclean was comparable to that of Walter Linse.

Linse, a leader of the anti-Communist "Free Jurists" Association, was abducted recently into East Berlin from West Berlin.

Donald Maclean, 38-year-old head of the Foreign Office American department, and Guy Burgess, 40, former second secretary at the British Embassy in Washington, disappeared on May 25 last year.

Herr Nuschke is head of an East German delegation of five which has brought a letter from the East German Government to the West German Government regarding German unity.

Anti-Communist demonstrators hurled tomatoes and leaflets at the delegation when they arrived in Bonn. Later a crowd of 3,000 collected outside their hotel.

100-374183

DAILY DISPATCH
London
Sept. 21, 1952

RE: DONALD DUART MacLEAN, ET AL
ESPIONAGE - R

78 NOV 6 1952

OFFICE OF THE LEGAL ATTACHE
AMERICAN EMBASSY
LONDON, ENGLAND

306

100-374183-A
NOT RECORDED
98 NOV. 3 1952

He May Have Clue to Lost Diplomats

Scotland Yard are trying to trace Mr. Jack Hewit, friend of MacLean and Burgess, the diplomats, who disappeared last year. Mr. Hewit, who shared a London flat with Burgess, is believed to have recently returned from holiday on the Continent, and he may be able to help the police in their search for the missing diplomats.

DAILY MAIL
London
10-8-52

RE: DONALD DUART MacLEAN, ET AL
ESPIONAGE - R

OFFICE OF THE LEGAL ATTACHE
AMERICAN EMBASSY
LONDON, ENGLAND
60 OCT 29 1952

INDEXED - 120
307

Long-Missing British Diplomat is Reported Traced to Italy

Newsman Discovers Plenty of Evidence But Misses Man

By Hugo Kuranda

ASOLO, Italy, July 2 (NANA-Jemnews).—Police I have spoken to in Asolo have no doubt that the Englishman at the Villa La Mura was Guy Burgess. I have no reason to suppose they are wrong. There is plenty of evidence here. I missed Burgess by some 72 hours. He disappeared suddenly—

Guy Burgess, missing British diplomat, has been reported traced to the frontier of Northeastern Italy. The vital clue to the whereabouts of the former Foreign Office employe, who disappeared with Donald MacLean, 13 months ago, was unearthed in London. Reporters were assigned to track down Burgess. This dispatch recounts what transpired.

After a mysterious telephone call to the local police had warned them of his presence in the vicinity.

When the message from London reached me in Rome, I telephoned to the Asolo police. I asked them if they could help me contact "an English friend of mine" living here—and gave them a full description of Guy Burgess without mentioning his name.

The police at once fired a succession of questions at me. Who was I? What did I want? Why did I believe my friend was in Asolo?

As I was attempting some harmless explanation, the girl at the Asolo telephone exchange suddenly broke into the conversation.

Operator Gives Clue.

"I know them," she said. "I have seen Mr. Burgess, but I have seen the lady. They live at the Villa—"

Before she could say any more the police officer interrupted her angrily, shouting: "Who told you to give information to the public?"

They were furious at the girl for giving away what they were trying to conceal.

I had learned enough to make me leave at once for Asolo. Asolo, though only 50 miles from Venice, is hard to get at. It was a long climb by hired car into the mountains beyond Treviso.

This time I found the officer in charge of the local police in person. He had obviously decided against any further attempts at concealment.

"We did have such an Englishman here," he told me. "We have many strangers here from time to time, who come to visit our poet, Robert Browning's home at Asolo, but this one was different from the rest of the English.

"He was thick-set, about 5 feet 8 inches high. He had a strong beard, and always wore a Panama Hat."

Identified From Clipping

I showed the officer a newspaper cutting with a photo of Burgess (who was clean-shaven when he left England). He studied it intently for some time, then with a pencil drew a beard on the picture.

"That's him all right. He stayed with English people, one of them a Mr. Samuel Langford, of London, who for the past six months has been living here in the Villa La Mura adjoining the Browning house.

"Four nights ago we received an anonymous phone call. It was a foreign voice. We were told to watch that stranger with the beard.

"When we checked up the following morning the man with the beard was not there. His name? Ah, but you must understand we are not notified about visitors who come only for a short stay."

The police officer chuckled. "But I dare say his presence here has been noted by the British. We

have living in Asolo British lady, Mrs. Freya Stark, who we know worked for the British intelligence service. She is warmly disposed towards Italy. We get on fine with her."

I went up the hill in blinding sunshine to the Villa La Mura. I was shown into Langford's study by an Italian maid who spoke perfect English.

Volunteers Information

Langford is a tall, red-haired man of about 35.

Without waiting for me to state my business he said:

"I am afraid I can tell you nothing about Guy. But he isn't here, nor has he been here. I think he is dead."

Pressed to explain himself, Langford finally said: "Well, he never was a Communist. I knew him very well and saw a lot of him when we worked together in London. That was before I came abroad. I am doing free lance journalistic work here in Italy, including photography, mainly for America."

"How do you know I have come to inquire about Guy Burgess?" I asked, quickly.

"Oh well!" Langford hesitated. "But everybody does.

"And the man with the beard the police say stayed with you until three days ago?"

Langford looked taken aback. "That was a friend from home. A colleague of mine. No, I really know nothing about Guy."

After a pause he asked: "What else did the police tell you about me?"

I called next at the house where the police said Mrs. Freya Stark, the famous explorer and authoress and former member of the British intelligence service, was staying.

The lady had just left for an unknown address.

Diplomats Traced.

Evidence that the missing British diplomats Guy Burgess and Donald MacLean may have traveled to Poland in a Polish ship from Dunkirk a few days after they were last seen in Brittany in May of last year has been obtained by German intelligence agents from a Communist agent arrested in Bremen.

The Germans were searching for members of the illegal eastern German Communist sabotage organization Wollweber in North German ports.

They picked up a Pole of German origin named Edmund Wegener whose job was to act as a secret courier between Communist agents in French, and German ports and Poland.

For these trips he traveled to and fro between Western Europe and Danzig on the Polish ship Warmia. He told the Germans that two Englishmen whose descriptions fitted those of Burgess and MacLean traveled on the Warmia from Dunkirk to Danzig in May 1951.

After questioning, the 50-year-old "salesman" made a full confession. He admitted working for the Wollweber spy ring, which is sending large supplies of machine guns, rifles and other armaments

— AP Wirephoto.

GUY BURGESS.

LONDON--DONALD MACLEAN AND GUY BURGESS, FOREIGN OFFICE OFFICIALS WHO DISAPPEARED WITHOUT TRACE A YEAR AGO, ARE BEING DISMISSED FROM THEIR POSTS. IT WAS ANNOUNCED TODAY.

THE TWO DIPLOMATS, KEY MEN IN THE FOREIGN OFFICE, LANDED AT ST. MALO, FRANCE, IN A CHANNEL STEAMER FROM ENGLAND LAST MAY 26 ON A VACATION.

THAT IS THE LAST AUTHENTIC WORD OF THEM.

5/19--N1116A

DELETED COPY SENT C.R. Mac Donald
BY LETTER JUN 22 1976
PER FOIA REQUEST.

NOT RECORDED
98 JUL 2 1952

WASHINGTON CITY NEWS SERVICE 309

MISSING DIPLOMAT REPORTED SEEN IN ITALY

By HUGO KURANDA, Daily Graphic Correspondent, Venice

GUY BURGESS, the missing British diplomat, is reported to have been seen at the Italian frontier town of Asolo, 40 miles north of Venice.

But when I called at the home there of authoress Freya Stark, a tall, grey-haired Englishman with a military moustache told me:

"Miss Stark is engaged and has nothing to tell you about Burgess."

The mystery deepened when I asked the man how he knew I called to inquire about Burgess.

"You told the maid." he replied, though I had not done so.

"May I ask your name?" I said. "Never mind, just a visitor," he answered.

While we were talking a smart Italian sports car stopped at the gate. Its driver, a woman, approached the man.

"Freya" is expecting you," he said, as the visitor brushed past.

She was Miss G' Murchie.

a blonde Englishwoman, aged around 45, who about a year ago rented the secluded Villa Pasini outside Asolo.

Her car had a Trieste number plate.

Trieste, adjoining Tito's Yugoslavia, is about 115 miles north-east of Asolo.

There was no reply to my ringing at poet Robert Browning's villa, which has been rented for the past six months by Mr. Sam Lanford and Mr. Brian Howard, both of whom had told me they knew Guy well.

K

LONDON--(FRIDAY)--A ZURICH DISPATCH TO THE LONDON DAILY EXPRESS SAID
TODAY THAT DONALD MACLEAN, ONE OF TWO BRITISH DIPLOMATS MISSING FOR
MORE THAN A YEAR, IS NOW LIVING IN PRAGUE, CZECHOSLOVAKIA.
    THE DAILY EXPRESS SAID IN A FRONT PAGE BANNERLINE STORY THAT ITS
ZURICH CORRESPONDENT HAD "PROOF" THAT MACLEAN WAS IN THE CZECH CAPITAL
AND THAT IT HAD BEEN ESTABLISHED THAT HE SENT 1,000 POUNDS ($2,800) TO
HIS MOTHER-IN-LAW IN LONDON AFTER WITHDRAWING THAT AMOUNT FROM A SMALL
SWISS BANK.
        6/5--EG835P

C.B. MacDonald

DELETED COPY SENT
BY LETTER JUN 22 1976
PER FOIA REQUEST

JUN 26 1952

61 JUL 1 1952

WASHINGTON CITY NEWS SERVICE

311

Where Colonel Pinto akes over

MOTIVES? ... MEANS?

A NUMBER of vital questions arising from the mystery of the two Foreign Office men remain unsolved after a year of continuous inquiry. These must be sifted and answered by Colonel Pinto before he can resume the trail. Perhaps the hardest to answer is—

WHY DID BURGESS GO WITH MACLEAN?

The life of Guy Burgess was well known to all of his friends. He liked a good time. He hated to take life seriously.

Most important of all, he barely knew Donald Maclean. They were contemporaries at Cambridge, but appeared to have had little contact throughout the years that followed.

No one saw them meet in London in the three weeks that Burgess stayed after his return from Washington.

When did they meet? What was said to make Burgess give up everything he had in England? What did Burgess learn in America that would make him telephone Lady Maclean and ask for her son's address?

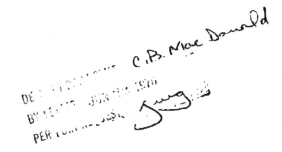

WHY DID BURGESS, A BACHELOR, LEAVE A NOTE, BUT MACLEAN SAY NOTHING TO HIS WIFE?

It is believed that Burgess left a letter—the letter that was altered—to prevent an alarm being raised. But, for some reason, it was not delivered. His friends went to M.I.5.

Maclean had two good reasons for leaving a note of farewell. It was his birthday and Mrs. Maclean and the family had planned a small party for him.

And he knew that his third child—his daughter, Melinda—was expected within a matter of days. Yet he walked out without a word. *What happened to make him do that?*

WHY DID BURGESS—

—a man not normally given to serious expression in his letters—write to a friend just before he came home from America:

> I am terrified that there may be a war. Very seriously for the first time. And soon. I sail on the Queen Mary

What had he learned that had terrified him? Was it something to do with his contact with Maclean?

DID THEY HAVE ANY MONEY WITH THEM?

Burgess certainly did. He took everything he could raise in ready cash. The total was something over £300.

He came back from America with two bundles of £1 notes. These he never touched; they were left in a closed suitcase in his flat for the whole of the three weeks.

One bundle totalled £125. The other was bigger, and contained about £150. Burgess explained them by saying he had made a little cash "in a black market dollar deal."

He withdrew Savings Certificates worth £50. Obviously, he intended to leave nothing behind.

313

THIS FAMOUS
INVESTIGATOR—
AND AUTHOR OF
'SPYCATCHER'
—HEADS A NEW
INQUIRY FOR
THE EXPRESS

The trail that led to Paris

By DONALD SEAMAN

There is nothing as yet to suggest that Burgess is behind the Iron Curtain... or even that he is still with Maclean'

YOU will assume—if you believe that the diplomats Burgess and Maclean have disappeared for political reasons—that I have been called in because of my knowledge of the art of counter espionage.

That experience, of course, will be of immense value to me. Every trick, every ruse I have learned in 34 years' work will be employed in my attempt to solve this absorbing mystery.

But I must tell you at once that the very nature of this inquiry—with one historic exception—is foreign to me.

Year-old trail

WITH that one exception my life of counter espionage has been devoted to the *prevention* of disaster—the disaster that only spies and agents can bring about.

In the Burgess and Maclean case I have to assume that the disaster has happened already.

Here I am taking up a trail a year old.

Here I have none of my former official powers.

Here I am on my own.

When I was first asked to investigate the disappearance of the two men, I had many doubts and misgivings. Chief among them was the fact that the trail I must take up is one year old. One year cold, too.

Why then have I accepted this case? When my misgivings were greatest I was given access to the findings of the Daily Express investigating teams, at home and abroad.

I was shown a mass of evidence, the product of a year's work : photographs, the reports of handwriting experts, names, addresses, facts that have never been disclosed.

Intention

IF you have studied with care the important document published on Page One of yesterday's Express and realised its implications — then you will know that the theorists must make a new start.

But for that letter from Burgess—withheld for a year

from the friend he wanted to receive it—we would not have known of Burgess's firm intention to break away from his old life and disappear.

This, and other details soon to be disclosed to you, indicated to me that the thing was possible. The inquiry could be undertaken, even now : and given luck—always a necessary weapon in my armoury—there is a chance of reaching a satisfactory conclusion.

Let me tell you why I stress the value of "luck" and "hunches" in an investigation

---

by Lieut.-Col. ORESTE PINTO

---

of this kind. I have worked on my hunches before, and many spies are long since dead because a hunch was right.

A hunch

THE one important case in my career of counter espionage which, like the Burgess and Maclean case, was *not* the prevention of disaster, was the tracking of a man *after* the event.

Christiaan Lindemans a Dutchman like myself, was a gorilla of a man. He was so broad you could never realise he stood 6ft. 2ins. in height.

All of us, and everyone in the Dutch underground, knew him as "King Kong."

I knew of him as a leader of that brave movement. He had done wonderful work during the occupation. He had helped a lot of people escape to us.

Then came Arnhem, and disaster. I had a hunch. Through another agent I captured later I learned that Lindemans had given the Germans all the plans two days before the airborne drop.

Lindemans was arrested and flown to England. He confessed : later committed suicide in a Dutch prison.

Now what do we know in this case? What are the circumstances from which such a hunch might spring?

WE KNOW the men have

left the country : *but I am keeping a completely open mind as to their whereabouts.*

On the evidence, I am inclined to the view that Donald Maclean IS in a country behind the Iron Curtain.

There is nothing whatever, to my mind at this stage, to show that Guy Burgess is with him, or, indeed, behind the Iron Curtain at all.

I have the evidence of his intimate friends, the evidence of his unchanging tastes and habits, his luxury - needing character.

There is nothing to show even after a year's investigation, that he was at any time politically suspect.

One word, at this stage, about the character of these two. There is evidence of physical unbalance.

It is a curious thing that from my 34 years in the ruthless world of counter espionage, plot and counter plot, 50 per cent. of the spies and traitors I have met have been similarly affected.

What is it that makes them spy ? What is it that makes them take up this dangerous, often poorly paid, life ?

I have given much thought to this. I think it must be the agony of mind, the constant mingling of excitement and terror, the brutal and ever present sense of fear.

Endless checks

AND now for the future. Already the great pressure by the Press throughout the free world —and this newspaper has taken the leading role—has served, in one way, to add to my difficulties.

The leads I must take up, the people I must see, the endless checks to be made—all these things are made harder for me from the outset because of that incessant pressure.

But we shall see. . . .

BURGESS drove south, heading for the Channel, that evening in May, one year ago. When he boarded the steamer Falaise at Southampton, he was accompanied by Donald Maclean.

Burgess had made a detour to Maclean's home near Westerham to pick him up.

They arrived, with minutes to spare. Maclean had no luggage except a briefcase. Burgess loaded his two suitcases on board, carried a black official briefcase with him.

They drank at the bar, but made no effort to mix with other passengers. They disembarked at St. Malo at six o'clock on the morning of May 26, and made their way into the port—carrying only their briefcases.

*   *   *

WHAT DID THEY DO BETWEEN THAT TIME AND 11.30 A.M. ? For those five and a half hours Maclean and Burgess vanished again.

At 11.30, it has been established, the two diplomats hailed St. Malo taxidriver Albert Gilbert, and asked him to drive them to Rennes in time to catch the 1.18 p.m. to Paris.

Gilbert covered the 45 miles' journey in 90 minutes. He was paid a 500-franc tip (roughly 10s.) over and above the fare of 4,500 francs.

Maclean and Burgess left him and walked towards the station.

*   *   *

Weeks later it was learned in Paris that two men, answering the description of the missing diplomats, had called at the Czech Embassy in Paris.

For obvious reasons—who could question Czech Embassy officials on the story?—the report remained unconfirmed.

THE STATION AT RENNES is the last positive clue that Colonel Pinto has to take up.

WHAT NOW? Colonel Pinto's progress reports

will appear only in the Daily Express

New Turn In The Missing
Diplomats Mystery

BURGESS &
MACLEAN
A Surprise
Decision

SE 47

DELETED COPY SENT C.B. Mac Donald
BY LETTER JUN 25 1976
PER FOIA REQUEST

RE: GUY DUART BURGESS, ET AL
     ESPIONAGE - R

SUNDAY DISPATCH
May 11, 1952

OFFICE OF THE LEGAL ATTACHE
AMERICAN EMBASSY
LONDON, ENGLAND

JUN 12 1952

315

Security Officials Strike Their
Names Off List Sent To Ports

By Sunday Dispatch Reporter

THE search for Guy Burgess and Donald Maclean, the Foreign Office men who disappeared after landing at St. Malo, France, from a cross-Channel steamer a year ago, has been called off.

Their names have been removed officially from the list of "suspected persons" compiled by the Government for use by immigration officers at every British port.

This does not mean that the two diplomats have been found.

It is an indication, rather, that the possibility of their return to Britain is considered so remote that further watch for them would be a worthless waste of time.

Have They Had Some News?

One question raised is : Has Whitehall received information which makes it certain that neither man will ever attempt to return, even if he is able to do so ?

The "suspect list" supplied to immigration officers contains the names of persons, both British and alien, believed to be connected with subversive political activities, or otherwise likely to endanger the country's security.

If any persons named in the list land in Britain the immigration officers have instructions to question them.

Possible reasons for the deletion of Burgess and Maclean from the list are:

The authorities concluded some little time ago that Burgess and Maclean are either alive the other side of the Iron Curtain or dead somewhere this side of it.

They consequently called off the search for them which previously was being carried out by the British and Western European security services.

Moscow Claim

Guy Francis de Moncy Burgess, aged 40, and Donald Duart Maclean, 38, his greatest friend, caught the cross-Channel steamer Falaise at midnight on May 25 last year.

They arrived at St. Malo at 6 a.m. next day and went ashore

Of their movements after that nothing is certain.

There were some Central European rumours — completely unconfirmed — that they had been seen in Moscow.

But all efforts to check on this have failed

3/6

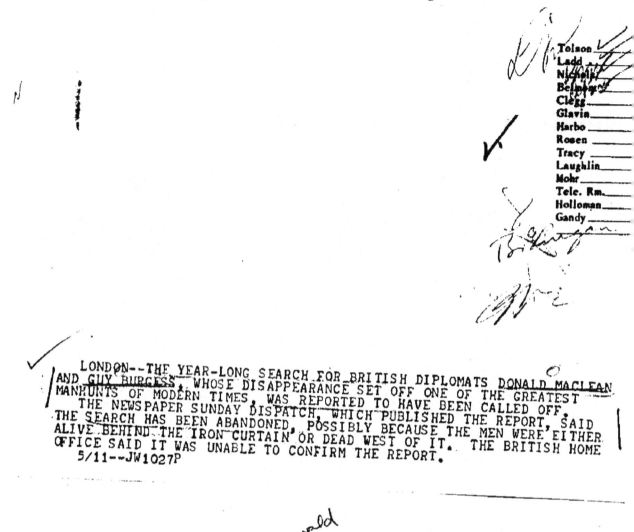

LONDON--THE YEAR-LONG SEARCH FOR BRITISH DIPLOMATS DONALD MACLEAN
AND GUY BURGESS, WHOSE DISAPPEARANCE SET OFF ONE OF THE GREATEST
MANHUNTS OF MODERN TIMES, WAS REPORTED TO HAVE BEEN CALLED OFF.
THE NEWSPAPER SUNDAY DISPATCH, WHICH PUBLISHED THE REPORT, SAID
THE SEARCH HAS BEEN ABANDONED, POSSIBLY BECAUSE THE MEN WERE EITHER
ALIVE BEHIND THE IRON CURTAIN OR DEAD WEST OF IT. THE BRITISH HOME
OFFICE SAID IT WAS UNABLE TO CONFIRM THE REPORT.
5/11--JW1027P

DELETED COPY SENT C.B. Mac Donald
BY LETTER JUN 29 1976
PER FOIA REQUEST

109-374183-A
RECORDED
12 1952

Search for Lost British Diplomats Reported Ended

LONDON, May 11 (AP).—The year-long search for British diplomats Donald Maclean and Guy Burgess, whose disappearance set off one of the greatest manhunts of modern times, was reported today to have been called off.

The newspaper Sunday Dispatch, which published the report, said the search has been abandoned, possibly because the men were either alive behind the Iron Curtain or dead west of it. The British Home Office said it was unable to confirm the report.

Maclean, 38, whose wife is the former Melinda Marling of New York, and his friend Burgess walked down the gangplank of a channel steamer at St. Malo, France on the morning of May 26 last year and vanished.

NOT RECORDED
145 MAY 19 1952

Times-Herald	
Wash. Post	✓
Wash. News	
Wash. Star	
N. Y. Times	
N. Y. Compass	

Date: 5-13-52

318

Ladd _____
Clegg _____
Glavin _____
Nichols _____
Rosen _____
Tracy _____
Harbo _____
Alden _____
Belmont _____
Laughlin _____
Mohr _____
Tele. Room _____
Nease _____
Gandy _____

LONDON--THE BRITISH FOREIGN OFFICE HAS DECIDED TO CLOSE THE CASE
OF MISSING DIPLOMATS DONALD MACLEAN AND GUY BURGESS WHO MAY HAVE GONE
BEHIND THE IRON CURTAIN, THE LONDON DAILY MAIL SAID.
   THE FOREIGN OFFICE HAS DECIDED "TO CEASE FURTHER ACTIVE INQUIRIES"
ABOUT THE TWO YOUNG MEN WHO DISAPPEARED MAY 25, 1951, THE NEWSPAPER
SAID.
   THE FOREIGN OFFICE REFUSED TO COMMENT ON THE NEWSPAPER REPORT.
3/6--JR 1000A

NOT RECORDED
126 MAR 19 1952

100-374183

WASHINGTON CITY NEWS SERVICE

319

Hello to Berlin

CHRISTOPHER ISHERWOOD, British-born but American-naturalised author and playwright, now in London from his home in sunny Santa Monica, California, is to visit Berlin soon.

It will be 47-year-old Isherwood's first return to the city since he gave up living there when Hitler

Isherwood

arrived on the scene. And Isherwood will have some explaining to do. Several of his old friends—especially his ageing landlady—have been astonished to find themselves, thinly disguised, in many of his stories.

Speaking with a soft American accent—he has lived in America for nearly 15 years — Isherwood told me that his consuming interest at the moment is Hinduism. He describes himself as a Vedantin — a man who accepts the philosophy of Hinduism without worshipping at its altars.

Working with a friend who is a Bengal monk, Isherwood has translated the Gita, which he describes as the Hindu "Bible." Next year he will accompany the monk on a pilgrimage to monasteries in India.

Huxley, Too

Isherwood tells me that his friends W. H. Auden, Aldous Huxley and John van Druten are also interested in Vedanta.

Though he has not done any work in collaboration with Auden for many years he has been working jointly with Van Druten. A play "I Am a Camera," written by Van Druten from an Isherwood short story is now being played on Broadway.

One thing Isherwood would not discuss: Guy Burgess, the missing diplomat. Though a friend of Burgess in the past he has not seen him since 1947. "I know nothing whatever about his disappearance," said Isherwood firmly.

"The Evening News"
London, England
January 23, 1952

54 FEB 27 1952

OFFICE OF THE LEGAL ATTACHE
AMERICAN EMBASSY
LONDON, ENGLAND

INDEXED · 96

NOT RECORDED
4 FEB 25 1952

C.B. MacDonald

100-374183

320

BURGESS AGAIN?
Czechs quit the world police
From PERCY HOSKINS: Paris, Sunday

THE Czechs today dropped out of Interpol—the 38-nation police crime-detection organisation. They gave no reason, but it is believed they resent inquiries about Burgess and Maclean, the vanished Foreign Office men, who were last seen in Prague.

Czechoslovakia was the last of the Communist States in Interpol. Bulgaria and Rumania quit a year ago.

The Burgess-Maclean and Pontecorvo affairs were regarded in the West as political rather than criminal matters, so that Interpol was not much concerned in the hunt for the men.

U.S. TO REJOIN?

But considerable pressure was used through other channels in an effort to get Czech co-operation in the inquiries.

Resignation of the last Red State opens the way for America to rejoin this police network which spreads its crook-trapping web across every country this side of the Iron Curtain.

Mr. J. Edgar Hoover, chief of the Federal Bureau of Investigation, withdrew his country's support last year because of Czech demands for repatriation of political refugees. This, he claimed, would be a violation of the commission's statute, which barred action against political offenders.

"Daily Express"
London, England
January 14, 1952

RE: DONALD DUART Maclean, et al
Espionage - R

OFFICE OF THE LEGAL ATTACHE
AMERICAN EMBASSY
LONDON, ENGLAND

Diplomats —a clue from Paris

By Stanley Bishop

FRENCH security police have told MI5 in London: "Watch out for news of your missing diplomats during the next few days."

Underground "grape-vine" tip to the Paris police HQ is that Christmas and New Year greetings to their relatives were posted by Donald Maclean and Guy Burgess in a small Czechoslovak town near Prague.

Last Summer

It is known that Maclean and Burgess went to Prague within a few weeks of their disappearance early last summer, when on a holiday cruise to France.

So far only one message from the two men has been authenticated.

That was from Burgess to a young woman in Paris. It was written in Prague, and said simply: "*We are all right. Do not worry. You will be hearing more later.*"

This woman was interviewed by French security officers. She is now in Barcelona, Spain.

C.B. MacDonald

File

NOT RECORDED
98 MAR 31 1952

"DAILY HERALD"
London, England
Jan. 2, 1952

Re: Donald Duart MacLean, et al
      Espionage — R

65 APR 2 1952

322

PARIS STORY OF BURGESS LETTER

From FRANK TOLE
PARIS, Wednesday.

WHILE the French Sûreté said to-day they had no further information about Burgess and Maclean, the missing diplomats, it is understood that a letter was received in France more than three months ago signed in the name of Burgess.

The letter had a Prague postmark and was addressed to a woman then living in Paris, and now in Spain. It said both men were well.

An official said to-day that the fact that a letter was addressed from Prague did not necessarily mean that either of the men was in Czecho-Slovakia.

C.B. Mac Donald

file

NOT RECORDED
9 MAR 61

"THE EVENING NEWS"
London, England
January 2 1952

Re: Donald Duart MacLean, et al
     Espionage - R   F85

65 APR 2 1952

OFFICE OF THE LEGAL ATTACHE
AMERICAN EMBASSY
LONDON, ENGLAND

323

Jessup and Eisenhower

Those who watched the Senate hearings on Ambassador Philip

Jessup detected a smear-Eisenhower undertone in that proceeding also. For Jessup is a Columbia University professor who not only served on Eisenhower's faculty, but received a letter from Ike defending him against the McCarthy pro-Communist attack.

Seated across the table from Jessup during the Senate hearings was a Republican who has vowed to stop Eisenhower and who has staked his entire political future on Taft—Owen Brewster of Maine (R).

It was Brewster who led the attack on Jessup inside the Senate committee, though privately admitting to other Senators that McCarthy hadn't proved his charges.

the Conservatives will NOT abolish socialized medicine. In fact, the Tories will expand public housing ... The infamous Polish steamship which carried spies (The S. S. Batory) has changed her dirty name. It is now the S. S. Cominform, a word originated by the Communists. She will sail the Baltic-Far East run ... The murder of the Pakistan Premier was a job by Russian Intelligence. The assassin's house revealed stacks of money, and the slain man carried large sums ... Nehru-Pakistan relations will not be ruptured by the assassination ... The search for McLain & Burgess, the missing British-Communist atomic spies, is considered a farce in high Intelligence circles. The two Red agents are in Russia. They took the Paris plane to Stockholm. They got aboard the Stockholm airliner to Helsinki (at the last moment) and were flown to the Soviet fortress of Porkalla Period

"Show Biz," by Abel Green and Joe Laurie, Jr., is to the theatrical arts what Churchill's memoirs are to international politics. No one can write history like the men who make it, and Variety has had as much impact on the making of "showbiz" history as in the printing of it. It is an enormous accomplishment to incorporate 50 years of the American Theatre authentically and authoritatively between the covers of a vastly entertaining book. It is even more difficult to capture the imagination of vivid, pulsating, and changing institutions, from the nickelodeon to color television, in the same volume, but Abel Green and Joe Laurie, Jr., have accomplished that miracle in "Show Biz."

The paced, straight-forward narrative style almost disguises the tremendous research and incredible scholarship upon which the exciting document is as

resign in December. She is slated for a Distinguished Service Medal ... Barkley wants Clement; Tobin wants John Sullivan, and Ed Flynn wants Fitzpatrick to succeed Bill Boyle. The darkest horse is Joe P. Kennedy ... The disillusioning story behind the rejection of the first tax bill was this: It raised taxes for Congressmen! ... The Internal Revenue investigations are centering around a New York lawyer, whose initials are J. H. .... The new tax bill adds up to a terrific impact on single women and bachelors ... Communists on the West Coast are plotting to picket General MacArthur when he visits Seattle .... The first tip that at least six top-ranking N. Y. police officials would be forced to resign was made over my microphone several weeks ago. That news was confirmed Saturday ... Another big shot un-

effectively shared as the anchorages of the George Washington Bridge, as racy as Belmont, as sparkling as Tiffany's, as sturdy as Manhattan's bedrock, this remarkable book will tower in the history of the American Theater like the Empire State over the City's skyline. "Show Biz" is more than the annals of the oldest and most vivid of the arts. It is a cardiograph of the Heart of the American people for the last fifty years.

The Defense Dept's Anna Rosenberg (now in Korea) may

Memos to the Editors

Josephine Baker, a Negro star, complained to authorities that she was discriminated against in the Stork Club and that she had been told I was in the place at the time.

I was not in the Stork Club at the time of the alleged discourtesy...I saw Miss Baker and her party arrive. I saw them seated at a table—about six or seven from where I sat with newspaper friends...I was told that they were served at least two rounds of drinks before any unpleasantness happened.

From where I sat everything seemed both normal and peaceful, and it did not occur to me that it would be otherwise...After nearly one hour, my friends and I left to attend the after-midnight preview of a new movie on B'way...I did not know there had been any incident until late the next afternoon when I received a complaint by telegram.

After 20 years on the air and almost 30 in the newspapers, I thought my record was crystal-clear when minorities are getting kicked around. It irritates me now to have to recite that record and disgrace myself with any defense. But I have to do it to remind some people whose memories are astonishingly short...The facts are that whenever I have been called upon in the case against man's inhumanity to man I was always easily recruited. For anyone to demand of me where I stand when ANY person is discriminated against in a public place, means that that person is no friend of mine.

I am appalled at the agony and embarrassment caused Josephine Baker and her friends at the Stork Club. But I am equally appalled at their efforts to involve me in an incident in which I had no part.

The following letter is from Walter White, executive secretary of the National Ass'n for the Advancement of Colored People:

"Dear Walter: I have examined the facts in the Josephine Baker-Stork Club incident. I have learned that you were unaware of what happened and did not know that she had been the subject of discourtesy.

"I know your record too well in your opposition to racial and every other kind of discrimination to believe that you would be a party to any insult to human dignity.—Walter White."

Last week I called attention to a notorious amendment attached to the Declaration of Peace with Germany. I gave it my entire newspaper col'm on Tuesday. Thanks to many thousands of readers who sent it to their Congressmen, that rotten amendment was defeated by a voice-vote in the U. S. Senate 2 days later...The highest taxes in our history are about to go into effect. The tax bill is so high that European money is running away to South America for fear it will have to pay part of the cost of defense. The truth is that if European troops are as timid as Europe's money, we are kidding ourselves if we think we have allies. The financial crisis is due in Europe because financial showdown with our allies is overdue in Washington...The new pay-as-you-go policy is mis-named. It means they *GO*—and we *PAY!*

By all means don't miss the current issue of Collier's...The entire number is packed with exciting articles by many leading American writers. It is a frightening preview of the next war... If every Russian could read it, that war could never happen. Some of the authors in it are Robert E. Sherwood, Hanson W. Baldwin, Lowell Thomas, Edward R. Murrow, Philip Wylie, Senator Margaret Chase Smith, Hal Boyle of the A.P., and mine is on page 39.

European currency is staggering. A whole series of devaluations is in the wind. The Yugoslavian dinar, the French franc and the British pound are in trouble...The big financial crisis over there may come in Feb....If Mr. Churchill wins, the Conservatives will *NOT* abolish socialized medicine. In fact, the Tories will expand public housing...The infamous Polish steamship which carried spies (The S. S. Batory) has changed her dirty name. It is now the S. S. Cominform, a word originated by the Communists. She will sail the Baltic-Far East run...The murder of the Pakistan Premier was a job by Russian Intelligence. The assassin's house revealed stacks of money, and the slain man carried large sums...Nehru-Pakistan relations will not be ruptured by the assassination...The search for McLain & Burgess, the missing British Communist atomic spies, is considered a farce in high Intelligence circles. The two Red agents are in Russia. They took the Paris plane to Stockholm. They got aboard the Stockholm airliner in Helsinki (at the last moment) and were flown to the Soviet fortress of Porkalla. Period...Sacha Machov, the former stage manager and dance director of the Sadler's Wells ballet, has committed suicide. In protest against the communization of the Czech National Opera.

"Show Biz," by Abel Green and Joe Laurie, Jr., is to the theatrical arts what Churchill's memoirs are to international politics. No one can write history like the men who make it, and Variety has had as much impact on the making of "showbiz" history as in the printing of it. It is an enormous accomplishment to incorporate 50 years of the American Theatre authentically and authoritatively between the covers of a vastly entertaining book. It is even more difficult to capture the imagination of vivid, pulsating, and changing institutions, from the nickelodeon to color television, in the same volume, but Abel Green and Joe Laurie, Jr., have accomplished that miracle in "Show Biz."

The paced, straight-forward narrative style almost disguises the tremendous research and incredible scholarship upon which the exciting document is as effectively shored as the anchorages of the George Washington Bridge. As racy as Belmont, as sparkling as Tiffany's, as sturdy as Manhattan's bedrock, this remarkable book will tower in the history of the American Theatre like the Empire State over the City's skyline. "Show Biz" is more than the annals of the oldest and most vivid of the arts. It is a cardiograph of the Heart of the American people for the last fifty years.

The Defense Dep't's Anna Rosenberg (now in Korea) may resign in December. She is slated for a Distinguished Service Medal...Barkley wants Clement; Tobin wants John Sullivan, and Ed Flynn wants Fitzpatrick to succeed Bill Boyle. The darkest horse is Joe P. Kennedy...The disillusioning story behind the rejection of the first tax bill was this: It raised taxes for Congressmen!...The Internal Revenue investigations are centering around a New York lawyer, whose initials are J. H....The new tax bill adds up to a terrific impact on single women and bachelors...Communists on the West Coast are plotting to picket General MacArthur when he visits Seattle...The first tip that at least six top-ranking N. Y. police officials would be forced to resign was made over my microphone several weeks ago. That news was confirmed Saturday...Another big shot underworld leader in Greater N. Y. is scheduled for execution. His last initial is "A"...Headline: "Taxes Raised Almost 12 Per Cent"...Oh, it's only money!

15,000

DETECTIVES

IN SEARCH
FOR THE TWO
DIPLOMATS

Relatives questioned
at Le Bourget

100 - 374183

C.B MacDonald

RE: UNKNOWN SUBJECTS,
ESPIONAGE - R

SUNDAY EXPRESS
JUNE 10, 1951
LONDON, ENGLAND

327

OFFICE OF THE LEGAL ATTACHE
AMERICAN EMBASSY
LONDON, ENGLAND

Mystery moves in Italy and Belgium

MORRISON TO TELL M.P.s TOMORROW

SEARCH FOR THE TWO MISSING BRITISH DIPLOMATS WAS SWITCHED LAST NIGHT TO POINTS IN NORTHERN FRANCE, ITALY, AND BELGIUM.

The diplomats—Donald Maclean, aged 38, and Guy Burgess, 40, both of the Foreign Office—have been missing since May 25.

In an arc of Western Europe stretching from Stockholm to Sicily, 15,000 detectives yesterday searched for them.

When their disappearance was first reported the search was concentrated on Paris. Last night, in

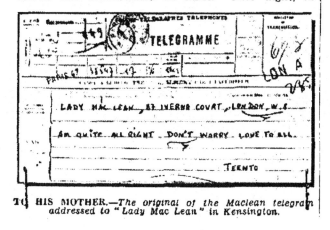

TO HIS MOTHER.—*The original of the Maclean telegram addressed to "Lady Mac Lean" in Kensington.*

328

2

addition to the French police, Rome and Brussels police went into action.

At first in Whitehall there was an inclination to think that the disappearance was merely a holiday escapade. Now a more serious view is being taken and as was said yesterday : " We are not excluding any theory."

THE CONTINENTAL POLICE ARE OF THE OPINION THAT THE MEN HAVE SEPARATED BY NOW.

Hamburg radio last night quoted an unconfirmed report by Bucharest radio that they had arrived in Prague. This is the first time the diplomats' disappearance had been mentioned by an Eastern European country.

The hunt went on in France following an all-day watch on the home of Mr. and Mrs. Scherres, Maclean's sister and brother-in-law. A caretaker said they had gone to Deauville to spend the week-end with friends.

But it was learned that Mr. and Mrs. Scherres had left for Le Bourget. They had booked seats on British European Airways Flight No. 340 for London.

Just as the plane was about to leave, French detectives told Airways officials that they wanted to question Mr. and Mrs. Scherres. The plane took off and the couple were accompanied by detectives to a private office on the airport.

M.I.5 chief acts

After one and three-quarter hours Mr. and Mrs. Scherres walked out with the detectives and told Airport officials they were now free to fly to London. Seats were reserved for them on the 5.30 p.m. plane.

Activity in Rome followed a Foreign Office statement that a telegram received in England by Burgess's mother had been sent from the Italian capital. Rome police later confirmed that such a cable had been sent.

Belgian police intensified their search after a report that the men had been seen in the Antwerp area.

In London it was announced yesterday that Mr. Morrison, Foreign Secretary, will make a statement in the House tomorrow on the disappearance of the men.

AND SIR PERCY SILLITOE, HEAD OF M.I.5, IS FLYING TO WASHINGTON TODAY TO CONFER WITH MR. EDGAR HOOVER, CHIEF OF THE F.B.I., ABOUT TIGHTENING UP SECURITY IN BRITAIN AND AMERICA.

Scotland Yard experts believe that telegrams purporting to be from the men—one from Burgess and two from Maclean—were sent after the news that they were missing had been published.

Both the Maclean telegrams—one to his home at Tatsfield, Surrey, where his wife is expecting a third baby.

329

```
M᷾ MAC LEAN MELINDA, BEACON SHAW, TATSFIELD NEAR WESTERHAM
                                          SURREY. ENGLAND
HAD TO LEAV UNEXPECTEDLY, TERRIBLY SORRY, AM QUITE
WELL NEWS DON'T WORRY DARLING. I LOVE YOU.
PLEASE DON'T STOP LOVING ME.
                                    DONALD
```

TO HIS WIFE.—*The original of the telegram, signed Donald, sent from Paris to Mrs. Maclean at Tatsfield.*

and the other to his mother in Kensington—were datelined Paris.

The telegram to Maclean's mother, Lady Maclean, was signed with a family nickname, "Teento."

It is known that Maclean was in Paris last Saturday and Sunday drinking with an English friend there.

Police in London now believe that the two Maclean telegrams were sent from Paris by another man or woman and that both Maclean and Burgess were in Rome when the other telegram was sent from there.

The Italian newspaper Il Tempo stated today that Guy Burgess travelled from Paris to Florence by car.

Sunday Express Correspondents and Agency messages.

330

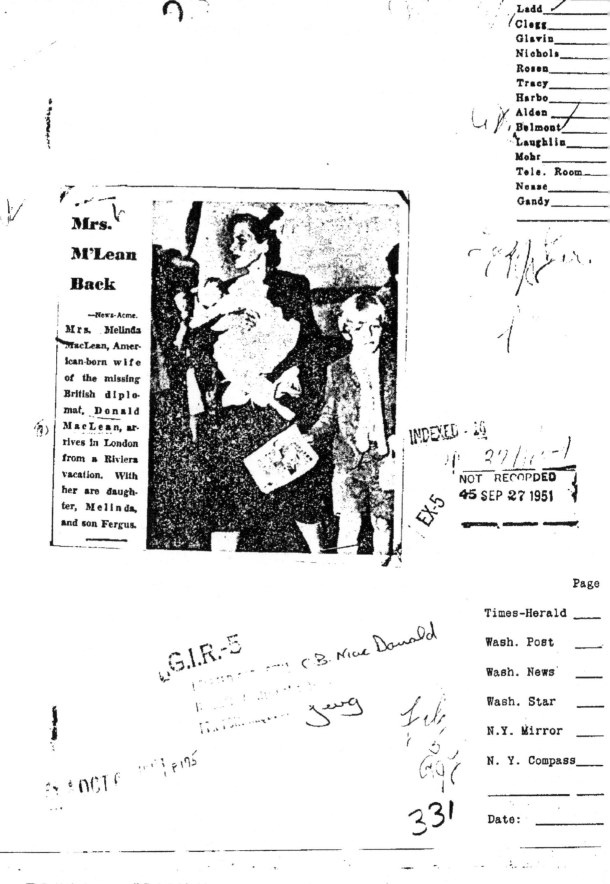

Mrs. M'Lean Back

—News-Acme.

Mrs. Melinda MacLean, American-born wife of the missing British diplomat, Donald MacLean, arrives in London from a Riviera vacation. With her are daughter, Melinda, and son Fergus.

INDEXED -

NOT RECORDED
45 SEP 27 1951

EX-5

G.I.R.-5

331

Villagers Insist that Macleans Are in Contact

'SECRET SERVICE' MAN HELPS

The village of La Garde Freinet, in which the missing diplomats were reported to be hiding, is just ten miles from Mrs. Maclean's villa. A Daily Mail reporter telephoned the village's only big hotel. Said the manager: "I know of the missing diplomats, naturally. But I have not seen them." The village is seething with rumours.

From RICHARD GREENOUGH

BEAUVALLON, Var, Thursday.

THERE appear to be good reasons for believing that Mrs. Melinda Maclean may recently have contacted her husband, the missing British diplomat, although she is quoted by the Sûreté, France's Scotland Yard, as having said today : " I have received no message from him. I don't know where he is."

The first indirect contacts, it is suggested here, may have been made through her sister and brother-in-law, Mr. and Mrs. Terrel, who live in Biarritz.

People in Beauvallon think these indirect contacts prompted Mrs. Maclean to come on holiday to the remote old château of La Sauvageonne—The Little Savage—set off the road two miles from here amid a forest of pine and cypress.

La Sauvageonne is owned by M. Gosselin. He is a close friend of the Terrels. And M. Gosselin is not entirely unconnected with France's Secret Service.

La Sauvageonne is an ideal hide-out, too, for any first meeting between the Macleans since May 25, the day when Mr. Donald Maclean so mysteriously disappeared with his fellow-diplomat, Mr. Guy Burgess.

Here with Mrs. Maclean are her mother, Mrs. Dunbar, her two married sisters, and her own three children. She has practically barricaded herself inside the château.

'Resembled her'

But since her somewhat sudden arrival on August 18 she has made three quiet trips up into the interior of this desolate region.

The latest was tonight. She is believed to be staying with friends at Grimaud, four miles from here. Her sister's car is parked at the Hotel Beausoleil there and a room —No. 7—is booked for "friends of M Gosselin."

Yesterday Mrs. Maclean went to the little village of La Garde Freinet, in the picturesque foothills of the Var, six miles from Grimaud.

She was driven there unostentatiously by M. Gosselin.

Today at La Garde Freinet I was told at the one and only hotel, the Auberge Sarrisine, by the owner, M. Jean Marquiset, that a woman resembling Mrs. Maclean had called there yesterday with a Frenchman, apparently expecting to meet somebody.

The police came today to inspect the hotel books and see who has been staying there recently. Callers at La Sauvageonne this afternoon were told that Mrs. Maclean and the whole family were "not at home, and we don't know where they are," but I could see them playing near the house.

M. Berthier, a local inhabitant who took his wife up to do some laundry for the household, told me his wife had a cup of coffee with Mrs. Maclean.

LA SAUVAGEONNE, *where Mrs. Melinda Maclean is staying with her mother, sisters, and children.*

Police guards

The château, with its steep, white walls rising out of the forest, is well guarded.

French police inspectors from Marseilles on direct orders from Paris are still on duty there although they remain invisible. And any unexpected and unwanted caller trespassing beyond the front driveway gate risks being attacked by ferocious dogs.

A close friend of the family today offered the most likely summary of events leading up to the present time.

Contact, the friend agrees, was possibly made between Donald Maclean and his wife through her sister and brother-in-law. There were indications that Maclean, and presumably Burgess, were then in the region. They had been reported seen in bars in Cannes and Nice.

The decision was then made for

Page THREE—Col. 6 ➡

'Macleans in Contact'

➡ **From PAGE ONE**

Mrs. Maclean to "plant" herself here in the hope that it might bring her husband out into the open to see his wife and children —the youngest born only a few days after his disappearance.

Mrs. Maclean and family arrived, but so did squads of French Police and Special Branch officers. A car-load of them met her at Nice while another car-load arrived simultaneously at the château.

"The resulting publicity probably frightened off Maclean, who planned to come to see his wife here," the friend said.

"But the authorities say Mrs. Maclean still believes it worthwhile for her to stay on. This belief may well be rewarded. It is quite probable that arrangements for a second rendezvous were made for a spot not far from here, possibly at La Garde Freinet, but that once again nothing happened."

The same friend reports that Mrs. Maclean and the whole family seem in good spirits.

'Detain them'

I understand that the French police who arrived here were alerted by Scotland Yard, and that they have been asked to detain Maclean and Burgess when found.

This has been confirmed from police headquarters at Nice. Late tonight there has been a further report that Maclean and Burgess had been seen at Cap Camarat, a remote community on the Mediterranean shore south of here.

One further interesting sideline to this mysterious case is that a French Minister recently told some friends in confidence in Cannes that, of course, "both British and French authorities know where Maclean and Burgess are and they are just awaiting the proper time to seize them."

'Found' Reports Denied by MI5

REPORTS yesterday that Burgess and Maclean had been found produced an unprecedented result, forcing an official statement out of Britain's M.I.5, most silent of silent services.

The Foreign Office was used as the mouthpiece for the denial, but facts it contained were issued with the approval of Sir Percy Sillitoe, who, as chief of M.I.5, is responsible only to the Prime Minister.

The statement said: "Reports published in a section of this morning's Press that Burgess and Maclean had been located have officially stated by the Foreign Office today to be without foundation."

It was added that the Foreign Office had checked that the source quoted in the reports (M.I.5) had made no statements such as those attributed to it.

333

Mrs. MACLEAN:
"I KNOW HE WILL RETURN SOME DAY"

French mayor says: He is not here

NEWS CHRONICLE REPORTER

MRS. MELINDA MACLEAN, wife of Donald Maclean, one of the two Foreign Office diplomats missing now for three months, said last night:

"I know my husband will come back some time."

Mrs. Maclean is on holiday at Beauvallon, near St. Tropez, on the Mediterranean coast of France. With her are her three children.

They arrived from England just 13 days ago and are staying at a villa called La Sauvageonne.

French Intelligence agents interviewed her there yesterday. They had been ordered to the villa by their Paris headquarters after a report that Donald Maclean had sent his wife a message.

It had been reported that Maclean (38) and Guy Burgess (40)—the other diplomat who vanished with him—had been located

Mrs. Maclean told the French agents that she did not know where her husband was at present. Then she stated her belief that he would still come back.

"Mrs. Maclean said that she has not heard from her husband since he disappeared," one of the agents said afterwards

Police guard

Another added that Mrs. Maclean had spent every night at the villa since she and her family arrived there. Continuous guard had been kept by the police.

Late last night the Surete Nationale said that though Maclean and Burgess had not been seen on French territory, "it is likely that Scotland Yard knows where they are. In any case, we are carrying on our look-out."

In a telephone interview, the Mayor of La Garde Freinet—the village nearest to where the Maclean family are staying—told me: "It is quite impossible for Mrs. Maclean to have met her husband here We have a population of only 700. Any new visitor would be noticed immediately."

Earlier, the Foreign Office, in the first of three statements through the day, said that reports of the diplomats having been found were unconfirmed.

Statement No. 2 was that the suggestion was "without foundation." But still the rumour persisted

The black car

A further report came from France that at 1.30 p.m. (G.M.T.) yesterday a black Hillman car had been seen leaving the villa.

It bore a registration plate of a type reserved for foreign tourists in France. Inside the car were a man and a woman. It left at such a speed that the passengers could not be identified.

Afterwards, it was found that two rooms had been booked at an hotel about six miles away. They were taken for "friends of M. Gosselin," owner of the villa La Sauvageonne.

A Foreign Office spokesman, in Statement No. 3, now said that suggestions that an official statement about Burgess and Maclean was to be issued within the next fortnight were also without foundation.

Embassies asked

"We do not know where they are," he stated. "All the authorities who might be able to assist have been asked to help in the search."

British Embassies and Consulates everywhere had been asked to supply any information which might reach them. This would apply to the Middle Eastern and South American States and Iron Curtain countries were also aware of the search.

This is how the mystery of the diplomats has built up so far:

They vanished on May 25 after landing from a week-end Channel cruise at St. Malo.

A few days later Burgess' mother received a telegram from him, handed in at Rome. Mrs. Maclean also had a telegram—from her husband and postmarked Paris.

When Mrs. Maclean and her children (including Melinda, who was born less than three weeks after the father's disappearance) left England for the South of France they were said to be going for a month's holiday

335

The Case of the Missing Story

First, we had the two missing British diplomats, MacLean and Burgess. Despite vague official denials it is generally believed they hauled a tidy lot of top Allied secrets to Moscow. But—no one knows. Despite Scotland Yard and the French Surete, it is still a mystery.

Then we had the matter of MacLean's missing wife. Vacationing on the Riviera, she "disappeared" for several days. Then, as quietly, she returned. For a day it was another mystery. Now? Well, we have yet to see any quote from Mrs. MacLean, at any time. Whether she met her husband secretly, as some say—no one knows. Score another zero for Scotland Yard and the Surete.

Now comes the case of the missing story. The Labor Party's London Daily Herald published a story based on alleged Secret Service information, that the two missing diplomats had been found. After strangely keeping silent for hours, the British Foreign Office announces there is no truth in the report.

Everybody likes a mystery, and this trick of making three mysteries out of one would be good fun—if the matter were not so serious. Over here, we suspect in Britain too, there is widespread feeling that the public has not been told "the half of it."

All British officials will say is that agents are hunting the diplomats. And all we need now is for the agents to disappear, too.

For awhile there was some argument over whether Sherlock Holmes was really dead, or still keeping bees in Sussex at an advanced age. From the looks of things we would say that he at least has left England.

Denies Report Missing Diplomats Were Found

By the Associated Press

LONDON, Aug. 30.—The Foreign Office denied today that British secret agents have located missing diplomats Guy Burgess and Donald MacLean.

William Ridsdale, head of the Foreign Office news department, said reports published in two London newspapers this morning were completely "without foundation." The Foreign Office kept silent for hours after the reports first appeared before issuing the denial.

Mr. Ridsdale conferred with top officials for an hour before making his comment.

He said the search for the two is exactly where it was before the stories were printed in today's issues of the Daily Herald and the Daily Express—in other words, Britain is still hunting for the two officials.

Stories Quote Agents.

The newspaper stories quoted agents of the British secret service as saying they had located the two diplomats who vanished without a trace last May 25.

Mr. Ridsdale said the agents claimed they made no such statements.

He refused to say whether the secret agents had made any statements at all which might indicate a new development in the Europe-wide search for the two Britons who were in a position to know many of the West's top secrets.

The London Daily Herald said the Foreign Office learned the whereabouts of the two after a three-month search by British agents and Western European police. It said MacLean had communicated with his American-born wife Melinda who is vacationing with their three children on the French Riviera.

The Herald is the newspaper of the governing Labor Party and has close government connections.

Whereabouts Not Indicated.

The Conservative Daily Graphic, in a dispatch from Paris, said the same story was current there and added that Mrs. MacLean had left her Riviera villa for a secluded spot in the Var Mountains, 50 miles away.

Neither story gave any hint where the men supposedly are and did not indicate one way or another whether they have disappeared behind the Iron Curtain.

The two men have been the quarry in one of the greatest manhunts of modern times since they disappeared May 25.

after frequent brushes with the police over traffic violations.

Foreign Secretary Morrison to the House of Commons there was no evidence they took any secret documents with them, but the government appeared concerned over possible betrayal of Western diplomatic secrets.

The government has made no progress reports on the search.

Traced to St. Malo.

The men were traced as far as St. Malo, France, and have been identified as passengers in a taxi which took them to Rennes. There the trail went cold.

Their families received telegrams from Paris and Rome, but the originals were not in the diplomats' handwriting.

McLean suffered a nervous breakdown while serving in Cairo, and there were suggestions in Parliament that heavy work in the American department brought on another one. Mr. Morrison said there was no evidence of this.

Another theory was that the two had gone off on a bender and were reluctant to return and face scandal.

INDEXED - 41

ex - 28

DEC 28 1951

G.I.R.-5

C.B. MacDonal

590CT5 1951

337

MI 5 KNOW WHERE LOST DIPLOMATS ARE

Mrs. Maclean has had news

By STANLEY BISHOP

DONALD MACLEAN and Guy Burgess, the diplomats who vanished on May 25, have been located.

Agents of MI 5 reported yesterday: We know where they are and what has happened since they landed at St. Malo.

American-born Mrs. Melinda Maclean, who is on a month's holiday on the French Riviera with her three children, has received a message from her husband, according to MI 5.

When I telephoned her villa, La Sauvageonne, at Beauvalon, near St. Tropez, last night, the local exchange reported: No reply.

The Foreign Office in London had no statement to make. And none is likely before next week, I learn.

The news means an end to a world-wide hunt which began whe· 38-year-old Maclean and 40-year-old Burgess stepped ashore from a week-end Channel cruise steamer at St. Malo.

The telegrams

A taxi driver reported driving them—without luggage—to Rennes to catch the Paris train.

Then began a comb-out of the French capital. But no clue was found until, some days later, came two telegrams—one to Burgess's mother and the other to Mrs. Melinda Maclean.

That from Burgess had been dispatched from Rome, Maclean's from Paris. The search spread through France to Italy . . . Switzerland . . Spain . . Belgium . . . from all over Europe came reports, rumours that the two men had been seen.

Scotland Yard men, Continental security forces, even holiday-makers, joined in the search.

But until yesterday there was no definite news.

DONALD MACLEAN

GUY BURGESS

339

Tolson
Ladd
Clegg
Glavin
Nichols
Rosen
Tracy
Harbo
Alden
Belmont
Laughlin
Mohr
Tele. Room
Nease
Gandy

(DIPLOMATS)

LONDON--THE LABOR GOVERNMENT DENIED A REPORT IN ITS OWN PARTY NEWSPAPER TODAY THAT MISSING BRITISH DIPLOMATS DONALD MACLEAN AND GUY BURGESS HAD BEEN FOUND.

THE THREE-MONTH OLD INTERNATIONAL MYSTERY--AND FEAR THE DIPLOMATS MIGHT HAVE DUCKED UNDER THE IRON CURTAIN--TOOK A CURIOUS TURN WHEN:

1. THE DAILY HERALD, OFFICIAL ORGAN OF PRIME MINISTER ATTLEE'S LABOR PARTY, SAID FLATLY THAT BRITISH MILITARY INTELLIGENCE AGENTS HAD LOCATED MACLEAN AND BURGESS.

2. WILLIAM RIDSDALE, CHIEF OF THE FOREIGN OFFICE PRESS DEPARTMENT, DENIED THE ENTIRE REPORT.

RIDSDALE ISSUED THIS STATEMENT:

"THE REPORTS APPEARING IN CERTAIN SECTIONS OF THE PRESS THAT MACLEAN AND BURGESS HAD BEEN LOCATED WAS OFFICIALLY STATED TO BE WITHOUT FOUNDATION. THE FOREIGN OFFICE HAS CHECKED THAT THE SOURCES QUOTED HAD MADE NO SUCH STATEMENTS AS THOSE ATTRIBUTED TO IT.

RIDSDALE'S STATEMENT WAS PROMPTED BY A STORM OF QUERIES FOLLOWING THE DAILY HERALD'S EXCLUSIVE STORY THIS MORNING. THERE WERE STILL SOME WHO BELIEVED, HOWEVER, THAT THE LABOR NEWSPAPER WAS "ON TO SOMETHING."

THE DAILY HERALD DID NOT GIVE THE SOURCE OF ITS STORY, BUT QUOTED AGENTS OF BRITAIN'S MI-5, THE MILITARY INTELLIGENCE SYSTEM.

THE NEWSPAPER SAID:

"AGENTS OF MI-5 REPORTED TO THE FOREIGN OFFICE YESTERDAY: WE KNOW WHERE THEY (MACLEAN AND BURGESS) ARE AND WHAT HAPPENED SINCE THEY LANDED AT SAINT MALO."

8/30--EG355A

WASHINGTON CITY NEWS SERVICE   340

Tolson
Ladd
Clegg
Glavin
Nichols ✓
Rosen
Tracy
Harbo
Alden ✓
Belmont ✓
Laughlin
Mohr
Tele. Room
Nease
Gandy

ADD DIPLOMATS, LONDON (255A)
IN ANOTHER DEVELOPMENT TODAY, FRENCH INTELLIGENCE AGENTS WERE
ORDERED TO QUESTION MRS. MELINDA MACLEAN AT HER RENTED RIVIERA VILLA
IN BEAUVALLON. THE ORDER WENT OUT AFTER THE DAILY HERALD CLAIMED SHE
HAD RECEIVED A FRESH COMMUNICATION FROM HER MISSING HUSBAND.
     A FRENCH GOVERNMENT SPOKESMAN IN PARIS SAID MRS. MACLEAN IS AND HAS
BEEN AT HER RIVIERA VILLA, DESPITE REPORTS THAT SHE HAD VANISHED LAST
FRIDAY AS MYSTERIOUSLY AS HER HUSBAND.
     THE FRENCH ORDER WAS ISSUED BEFORE THE FOREIGN OFFICE DENIAL IN
LONDON.
     THE HERALD DID NOT SAY WHEN OR WHERE THE DIPLOMATS HAD BEEN FOUND.
     A FOREIGN OFFICE SPOKESMAN AT THE REGULAR MID-DAY PRESS CONFERENCE
SAID THE DAILY HERALD APPARENTLY HAD DEPENDED ON AN OFFICIAL OF MI-5
AS ITS UNNAMED SOURCE.
     "IS THE SEARCH CONTINUING?" A NEWSMAN ASKED.
     "WELL, IN THE SENSE THAT WE HAVE ASKED ANY AUTHORITIES WHO COME
ACROSS THEM TO REPORT THAT FACT," THE SPOKESMAN REPLIED.
     THE DIPLOMATS COULD NOT BE ARRESTED OR BROUGHT BACK TO BRITAIN
FORCIBLY, THE SPOKESMAN SAID. THEY HAVE BEEN CLEARED OF ANY CHARGE
OF TAKING OFFICIAL SECRETS OUT OF THE COUNTRY AND THERE ARE NO
CRIMINAL CHARGES AGAINST THEM, HE EXPLAINED.
                                             /30--CM1000A

G.I.R.-5

INDEXED - 1
EX-5

WASHINGTON CITY NEWS SERVICE   341

Tolson _____ ✓
Ladd _____ ✓
Clegg _____
Glavin _____
Nichols _____
Rosen _____
Tracy _____
Harbo _____
Alden _____ ✓
Belmont _____ ✓
Laughlin _____
Mohr _____
Tele. Room _____
Nease _____
Gandy _____

ADD DIPLOMATS, LONDON (409P)
EARLY EDITIONS OF FRIDAY'S HERALD NOTED THE FOREIGN OFFICIAL
DENIAL BUT REPEATED THAT THE NEWSPAPER KNEW WHERE THE MISSING MEN ARE.
A FIVE-PARAGRAPH ITEM SAID THE HERALD HAD SENT THE FOREIGN OFFICE
A DAY-TO-DAY ITINERARY OF THE JOURNEY MADE BY THE MISSING DIPLOMATS,
INCLUDING INFORMATION ON THEIR PRESENT WHEREABOUTS. THESE DETAILS,
HOWEVER, WERE NOT PUBLISHED.
     THE HERALD REPORT STRENGTHENED A WIDESPREAD BELIEF THAT THE DENIAL
WAS A "DIPLOMATIC" ONE -- TRUE ONLY IN THE SENSE THAT THE TWO HAD HAD
NOT BEEN "LOCATED" IN SUCH A WAY THAT THEY COULD BE REACHED AT WILL.
     3730--GB 127

C.B. MacDonald
BY LETTER JUN 22 1976
PER FOIA REQUEST

WASHINGTON CITY NEWS SERVICE   342

Tolson _____
Ladd _____
Clegg _____
Glavin _____
Nichols _____
Rosen _____
Tracy _____
Harbo _____
Alden _____
Belmont _____
Laughlin _____
Mohr _____
Tele. Room _____
Nease _____
Gandy _____

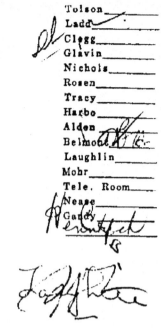

ADD DIPLOMATS, LONDON
    SOME RELIABLE AUTHORITIES BELIEVED THE TWO WHO DISAPPEARED FROM
LONDON LAST MAY 25 WENT TO CZECHOSLOVAKIA, REMAINED THERE FOR SOME
TIME, AND MAY STILL BE IN THAT COUNTRY.
    A BRITISH FOREIGN OFFICIAL FORMALLY DENIED A STORY SAYING MILITARY
INTELLIGENCE AGENTS HAD "LOCATED" THE DIPLOMATS.
    BUT THERE WAS A WIDESPREAD FEELING THAT THE DENIAL WAS A "DIPLOMATIC"
ONE, WHICH MIGHT BE ACCEPTED ONLY IN THE SENSE THE TWO MEN WERE
NOT "LOCATED" IN SUCH A MANNER THEY COULD BE REACHED AT WILL.
    5/30--GM127P

WASHINGTON CITY NEWS SERVICE   343

2 Diplomats Found, Says British Paper

LONDON (Thursday), Aug. 30 (U.P.).—British intelligence officers have found the two missing British Diplomats, Guy Burgess and Donald MacLean, after a three months' search of western Europe, the London Daily Herald reported today.

The newspaper, organ of the Labor Party, said intelligence agents informed the Foreign Office yesterday they had traced the movements of the two men since they walked off a channel steamer at a French port, May 25, and vanished.

The newspaper said Mrs. MacLean, now on the French Riviera, had received a message from her husband, but it gave no further details. Mrs. MacLean's housekeeper, Sylvia Bettfield, said at their country home that she knew nothing of such communication.

Yard Is Noncommittal

Scotland Yard said it could neither confirm nor deny the report. One yard official said: "This is not our province. It is purely a foreign office affair."

No other London morning newspaper carried the story.

The two diplomats walked down the gangplank of the channel steamer Falaise at St. Malo, France, and vanished.

Their disappearance brought down a storm around the head of the Foreign Secretary in the House of Commons and sent Britain's Chief of Intelligence to Washington to talk with J. Edgar Hoover.

Many jumped to the conclusion it was another case of defection to Communism and that the two men had fled behind the Iron Curtain. But there was no concrete evidence.

No Bodies Turned Up

Another theory was that one or both of the men might be dead, but no bodies turned up.

A third theory was the men had thrown over their careers as the result of a "bender." Burgess, 40, a heavy-drinking bachelor, had been recalled from Washington because of a series of scrapes over fast driving. MacLean, 38, was worried over the expected birth of a third child.

no clues to their disappearance. The case was revived last week when Chicago-born Mrs. MacLean went to the Riviera for a vacation.

FRENCH ARE TO SEE Mrs MACLEAN

FRENCH intelligence agents in Beauvallon were ordered today to question Mrs Maclean about the reported receipt of a message from her husband, Donald Maclean, one of the missing British diplomats.

The order was given by headquarters in Paris.

Beauvalion agents told BUP that they would immediately call on Mrs Maclean, who has been holidaying in the district since August 17.

A spokesman for the agents said that she had spent every night at her villa since her arrival. He added that the French Intelligence was aware of every movement made by her.

Meanwhile in London Foreign Office officials issued a statement today denying that both missing diplomats, Maclean and Guy Burgess, had been found and that their whereabouts were known to MI5.

A spokesman emphasised that the search was being continued and every piece of evidence sifted.

All British Embassies and consulates. Including those behind the Iron Curtain and in South America, have been warned of the search.

French will question Mrs. Maclean

BEAUVALLON (Southern France), Thursday.—French intelligence agents here were ordered by their Paris headquarters to-day to question Mrs. Melinda Maclean about the reported receipt of a message from her husband, the missing diplomat, Donald Maclean.

An official of an intelligence unit said that a call would be made on Mrs. Maclean immediately.

Mrs. Maclean and her children arrived at Beauvallon on August 17.

There have been reports that she had disappeared from her villa for several days, but the Intelligence Units spokesman said that she had spent every night at the villa.

Phone removed

Mrs. Maclean was there last night as usual, he said, and added: "We know where she is at all times."

People who telephoned Mrs. Maclean's villa to-day were told that the telephone had been removed.—Reuter.

In London: The Foreign Office to-day denied reports that Donald Maclean and Guy Burgess had been found.

"There was no foundation," said a spokesman, "for the suggestion that the Foreign Office were about to make a statement."

He added that the Foreign Office had checked with a source to which statements had been attributed and had found that no such statements had been made.

The search is going on, and is not confined to Western Europe.

DIPLOMATS:

RIDDLE

GROWS

Whitehall Rejects

'Found' Report, But

Mrs. Maclean

Makes A Secret Trip

FRENCH POLICE ON GUARD AT HOLIDAY VILLA

By HAROLD WALTON,
"Evening News" Foreign Editor

WHAT LIES BEHIND THE NEW MYSTERY OF DONALD MACLEAN AND GUY BURGESS, THE MISSING FOREIGN OFFICE DIPLOMATS?

To-day, after conferences between Whitehall officials and security chiefs lasting an hour and a quarter, the Foreign Office issued a statement denying reports which had circulated in London since early morning that both of the missing men had been found.

Nevertheless, there is a growing conviction in many quarters that we are on the eve of solving this mystery, which has puzzled all Europe since the two men left England by the St. Malo steamer on May 25.

To-day from the Villa Sauvageonne, near St. Tropez, on the French Riviera, where she has been on holiday, Mrs. Melinda Maclean, Donald Maclean's wife, left on another mysterious journey.

To an *Evening News* reporter who asked where she had gone a friend made this reply: "She has gone to visit her husband at a village in the Var Department."

RENDEZVOUS
Called Off?

There was no hedging on this statement, although no further details were given.

But from inquiries elsewhere it soon became clear that Mrs. Maclean had gone to the village of La Garde Freinet, high up in the lonely mountains of Maures, 20 miles inland from St. Tropez.

Here, according to local gossip, Donald Maclean is now living.

If this is true it explains the previous visit Mrs. Maclean made to this village.

It explains those early reports which filtered down from the mountains to journalists in

Riddle of Missing Diplomats

Continued from Page 1

Cannes and Nice that Donald Maclean made a rendezvous to meet his wife near La Garde Freinet on August 23, and that although his wife left her villa in search of him for two whole days he called off the appointment at the last moment because of the publicity which her movements had aroused.

To-day, as excitement on the Riviera grew at the reports that Donald Maclean had been found, there was intense police activity at the Villa Sauvageonne.

French Intelligence agents, on instructions from their Paris headquarters, surrounded the house and no one was allowed near.

The police tried to make contact with Mrs. Maclean herself to discover whether the message she had received from her husband was genuine or not.

All that the police would say was that they had no information officially that Donald Maclean had been found.

Meanwhile, what was happening in London?

The reports that M.I.5 had located not only Maclean but also Guy Burgess (of whom there is no other news whatsoever) were published in one or two morning newspapers.

At four o'clock Foreign Office officials were roused from their beds to investigate.

Their investigations lasted several hours.

Soon after breakfast the Security authorities were brought in.

Hour after hour the talks went on.

Then, soon after 11 a.m., this official statement was issued:

Reports published in a section of this morning's Press that Burgess and Maclean had been located were officially stated by the Foreign Office to-day to be without foundation.

It was added that the Foreign Office had checked that the source quoted in the reports had made no such statements as those attributed to it.

C. F. Melville, the "Evening News" Diplomatic Correspondent, makes this comment on the statement:

Although issued by the Foreign Office the statement really comes from the Security authorities.

It is they who have informed the Foreign Office that they have nothing to substantiate the reports that Burgess and Maclean have been found.

I gather that every possible clue, even the most fantastic, is taken up by the security authorities and investigated in case it might lead to some new facts which would help to solve the mystery.

The view in official quarters therefore stands as it did before: that there are no hard facts to go on, and it is not possible to say where the two men are or even whether they are dead or alive.

The investigations by the British Security authorities, in co-operation with their opposite numbers in all the Western European countries, are continuing.

349

C.B. MacDonald

DELETED COPY SENT
BY LETTER JUN 22 1976
PER FOIA REQUEST

LONDON (THURSDAY)--THE DAILY HERALD REPORTED TODAY THAT GUY BURGESS
AND DONALD MACLEAN, BRITISH DIPLOMATS MISSING SINCE MAY, HAVE BEEN
LOCATED.

8/29--WO1027P

ADD DIPLOMATS, LONDON
    THE NEWSPAPER, ORGAN OF THE LABOR PARTY, SAID GOVERNMENT
INTELLIGENCE TOLD THE FOREIGN OFFICE YESTERDAY IT HAD TRACED THE
DIPLOMATS' MOVEMENTS SINCE THEY LANDED IN FRANCE MAY 25.
    IT SAID MRS. MACLEAN HAD RECEIVED A MESSAGE FROM HER HUSBAND BUT
GAVE NO DETAILS. MRS. MACLEAN IS NOW VACATIONING ON THE RIVIERA.
8/29--WO1029P

100-374163-A
NOT RECORDED
145 OCT 4 1951

52   1951

WASHINGTON CITY NEWS SERVICE

350

Tolson _____
Ladd _____
Clegg _____
Glavin _____
Nichols _____
Rosen _____
Tracy _____
Harbo _____
Alden _____
Belmont _____
Laughlin _____
Mohr _____
Tele. Room _____
Nease _____
Gandy _____

Guy Burgess
Donald MacLean

A STATE DEPARTMENT SPOKESMAN SAID HE HAD "NO INFORMATION" ABOUT A
LONDON DAILY HERALD REPORT THAT TWO MISSING BRITISH DIPLOMATS HAVE
BEEN FOUND.

THE FBI DECLINED COMMENT. INFORMED SOURCES SAID THE AGENCY HAD
RECEIVED NO WORD OF THE REPORTED DISCOVERY OF THE WHEREABOUTS OF THE
BRITONS.

8/29--WO1140P

DELETED COPY SENT   C.B. MacDonald
BY LETTER JUN 22 1976
PER FOIA REQUEST

100-37483-A
NOT RECORDED
145 OCT 4 1951

6 OCT 6 1951

WASHINGTON CITY NEWS SERVICE   351

Tolson_____
Ladd_____
Clegg_____
Glavin_____
Nichols_____
Rosen_____
Tracy_____
Harbo_____
Alden_____
Belmont_____
Laughlin_____
Mohr_____
Tele. Room_____
Nease_____
Gandy_____

Guy Burgess
Donald Maclean

ADD DIPLOMATS, LONDON
THE DAILY HERALD GAVE NO FURTHER DETAILS.
THE TWO DIPLOMATS HAD WALKED DOWN THE GANGPLANK OF THE CHANNEL STEAMER
FALAISE AT ST. MALO, FRANCE, AND VANISHED.
THE CASE WAS REVIVED LAST WEEK WHEN AMERICAN-BORN MRS. MACCLEAN
WENT TO THE RIVIERA FOR A VACATION. THERE WERE REPORTS SHE HAD
"DISAPPEARED" AND THERE WAS SPECULATION SHE HOPED TO FIND HER HUSBAND.
BUT A SOURCE CLOSE TO MRS. MACLEAN SAID LATER SHE NEVER LEFT HER
VILLA AND SUGGESTED THAT THE REPORT OF HER DEPARTURE MIGHT HAVE BEEN A
RUSE TO THROW NEWSMEN OFF THE TRACK.
8/29--W01120P

DELETED COPY SENT C.B. Mac Donald
BY LETTER JUN 22 1978
PER FOIA REQUEST.

100-34183-A
NOT RECORDED
145 OCT 4 1951

61 OCT 6 1951

352

MRS. MACLEAN, WIFE OF 'LOST' DIPLOMAT, BACK

Returns to Riviera Villa and Children

BEAUVALLON, France, Aug. 26 (AP)—Mrs. Melinda MacLean, wife of a missing British diplomat, apparently had returned to her villa here today. But she and police remained secretive about her movements.

Correspondents in this small French Riviera resort were not permitted access to the villa which Mrs. MacLean has rented, but a feminine voice—evidently a friend or a housekeeper—was heard telling the MacLean children to awaken their mother.

Shortly afterwards, two cars filled with persons left the villa for a short drive along the coast. Mrs. MacLean and two of her children apparently were in one of the cars.

Mrs. MacLean's husband, Donald MacLean, and Guy Burgess, a foreign office colleague, disappeared some months ago. Fear was expressed they had gone over to the Russians.

Chicago-born Mrs. MacLean came to the French Riviera on Aug. 17. For the last three days she had not been seen in her villa. There had been speculation that a reunion with her husband might result from her trip here. There have been many rumors—none verified—that MacLean had been seen in this area.

102-374183-A

RECORDED

9-21-51

Page

Times-Herald ✓

Wash. Post

Wash. News _____

Wash. Star _____

N.Y. Mirror _____

N. Y. Compass _____

DELETED COPY SENT C.B. Mac Donald
BY LETTER JUN 22 1970
PER FOIA REQUEST

Date AUG 27 1951

Tolson
Ladd
Clegg
Glavin
Nichols
Rosen
Tracy
Harbo
Belmont
Mohr
Tele. Room
Nease
Gandy

BEAUVALLON, FRANCE--MRS. LEINDA MACLEAN, AMERICAN WIFE OF MISSING
BRITISH DIPLOMAT DONALD MACLEAN, HAS LEFT HER VILLA HERE FOR AN
UNDISCLOSED DESTINATION, IT WAS REVEALED TONIGHT.
    POLICE DECLINED TO REVEAL WHERE SHE MIGHT HAVE GONE. SHE HAD BEEN
HERE SINCE AUG. 17 FOR WHAT SHE SAID WAS A VACATION. SHE WAS
SAID TO HAVE LEFT TWO DAYS AGO.
    HOWEVER, HER MOTHER AND TWO CHILDREN STILL ARE AT THE VILLA.
    MRS. MCLEAN'S HUSBAND AND ANOTHER DIPLOMAT, GUY BURGESS,
DISAPPEARED MYSTERIOUSLY MAY 25, AND THERE WERE UNCONFIRMED REPORTS
THEY HAD FLED BEHIND THE IRON CURTAIN.
    8/24--JW504P

later report rec'd that she had not disappeared

DELETED COPY SENT C.B. macDonald
— BY LETTER JUN 23 1976
PER FOIA REQUEST

INDEXED - 24

NOT RECORDED
149

EX-176

76 SEP 15 1951

WASHINGTON CITY NEWS SERVICE

DATE:

354

ALAN MACLEAN QUITS FOREIGN OFFICE

By Daily Mail Reporter

THE resignation, announced yesterday, of 27-year-old Mr. Alan Maclean—younger brother of Donald Maclean, the missing diplomat—from the Foreign Office was described as "tragically unfortunate" by his mother, Lady Maclean. She said at her country home at Penn, Buckinghamshire:

"Alan could not have gone on in the Foreign Office. He did not have a permanent position there.

"The pity is that the post he was to have taken in America would have made him a permanent member of the foreign service. But you can imagine what it would have been like after this unfortunate business of his brother. It was simply not to be thought of."

Mr. Alan Maclean, a temporary officer of the foreign service for four years, said: "I resigned of my own volition. I have no definite plans for the future.

"I have no information whatever as to the whereabouts of my brother."

Mr. Morrison, Foreign Secretary, accepting his resignation, suggested that the normal month's notice should be extended by a further month until September 30.

The Foreign Office letter takes note of the fact that Mr. Maclean resigned on the understanding that there is no suggestion that he is in any way implicated in the disappearance of his brother, or that he believed him to have unwittingly taken any steps injurious to the security or interests of the country.

Mr. Maclean said the extra time offered by Mr Morrison was a "welcome and generous gesture."

DONALD DUART MacLEAN, et al
ESPIONAGE - R

DAILY MAIL
AUGUST 22, 1951
LONDON, ENGLAND

100 - 37483 - 1

NOT RECORDED
45 SEP 25 1951

DELETED COPY SENT   C.B. MacDonald
BY LETTER JUN 22 1976
PER FOIA REQUEST

355

6-20
Tolson ___
Ladd ___
Clegg ___
Glavin ___
Nichols ___
Rosen ___
Tracy ___
Harbo ___
Belmont ___
Mohr ___
Tele. Room ___
Nease ___
Gandy ___

LONDON--THE FOREIGN OFFICE ANNOUNCED THE RESIGNATION FROM THE
DIPLOMATIC SERVIE
DIPLOMATIC SERVICE OF ALAN MACLEAN, YOUNGER BROTHER OF MISSING DIPLOMAT
DONALD D. MACLEAN.
  DONALD MACLEAN AND GUY BURGESS, KEY BRITISH DIPLOMATS, DISAPPEARED
IN CIRCUMSTANCES STILL MYSTERIOUS ON MAY 25 AFTER ARRIVING IN FRANCE
FROM LONDON.
  ALAN MACLEAN HAS BEEN SERVING AS A TEMPORARY OFFICER IN THE
FOREIGN SERVICE FOR FOUR YEARS.
  FOREIGN SECRETARY HERBERT MORRISON, ANNOUNCING THE RESIGNTION,
SAID IT DID NOT IMPLICATE MACLEAN IN HIS BROTHER'S DISAPPEARANCE AND
WAS NOT FOR SECURITY REASONS.
                 8/21--GE1236P

INDEXED - 24   100-374183A -
                      NOT RECORDED
EX-76   249

76 SEP 15 1951   WASHINGTON CITY NEWS SERVICE
                  DATE: 356

Tolson
Ladd
Clegg
Glavin
Nichols
Rosen
Tracy
Harbo
Belmont
Mohr
Tele. Room
Nease
Gandy

PARIS--FRENCH SECRET SERVICE AGENTS ARE MAINTAINING A ROUND-THE-CLOCK
WATCH ON THE RIVIERA VACATION VILLA OF MRS. MELINDA MACLEAN IN HOPE
THAT HER MISSING BRITISH DIPLOMAT HUSBAND MAY SHOW UP THERE
DONALD MACLEAN AND GUY BURGESS, ANOTHER BRITISH FOREIGN OFFICE
DIPLOMAT, HAVE BEEN MISSING SINCE MAY. REPORTS THAT THEY MADE THEIR
WAY THROUGH THE IRON CURTAIN TO SOVIET TERRITORY HAVE NEVER BEEN
CONFIRMED.
          8/21--VO435P

Mrs. Donald Maclean

DELETED COPY SENT   C.B. MacDonald
BY LETTER JUN 22 1976
PER FOIA REQUEST

INDEXED - 106   100 = 374/185 A

G.I.R.-5   EX. - 28   NOT RECORDED
                           17 SEP 27 1951

59 OCT 4 1951

WASHINGTON CITY NEWS SERVICE

DATE: 357

Missing Diplomat's Wife Leaves England For French 'Holiday'

By the Associated Press

LONDON, Aug. 17.—The wife of a missing British diplomat left by air for France today—with the approval of the Foreign Office—on what she described as "a holiday."

She is Mrs. Melinda MacLean, whose husband, Donald, disappeared with a Foreign Office colleague, Guy Burgess, after a mysterious trip to France May 26. The Foreign Office has acknowledged the possibility that the pair may have gone over to Russia.

The trip immediately aroused speculation that there might be some hope on the part of Mrs. MacLean and the Foreign Office that her husband will seek her out in France.

She insisted, however, that her only purpose was to have a vacation.

Three Children in Party.

With Mrs. MacLean were her three children, Fergus, 7; Donald, 4, and Melinda, 2 months old, who was born 3 weeks after her father vanished. Her mother, sister and 6-year-old nephew also were in the party.

MacLean, 38, was head of the foreign office's American department. Burgess, 40, was a former official of the British Embassy in Washington, where he had access to secret dispatches.

They were last seen landing from an excursion boat in St. Malo, France. They had boarded it in Southampton.

There have been dozens of reports since then placing them in widely separated parts of France, Belgium and Italy. In every case police investigations have come to nothing.

INDEXED - 38

EX - 15

100-374183-a

Page

Times-Herald _____

Wash. Post _____

Wash. News _____

Wash. Star a 3

N.Y. Mirror _____

Date: 8-12-51

DELETED COPY C.B. MacDonald
BY LETTER JUN 22 1976
PER FOIA REQUEST

358

76 OCT 23 1951

Two 'Missing' British Envoys Rumored Slain

By JOHN O'DONNELL

The best whispered thriller in Washington in many a year is the story of what reportedly happened to the two British diplomats who vanished loaded down with the top secret atom bomb information that Pal Joey in the Kremlin was thirsting to get.

The current yarn is that either British information agents or our own American intelligence operators knew the plan of the boys in advance, trailed them when they slipped away from London and then—in the best tradition of the movies—quietly eliminated both before either had a chance to give their secrets to Russian agents behind the Iron Curtain.

The story is that we or the British, or both working together, caught up with the two traitors on the French-Italian Riviera border in a modest hotel room, shot them both thru the head and then effectively disposed of the bodies.

At least it sounds plausible, more so perhaps than does that peculiar Christmas eve assassination of France's Adm. Darlan, at Algiers in 1942 after the French naval commander had made his deal with Gen. Eisenhower and then complained that the Americans were about to toss him aside "like a lemon that had been squeezed dry."

Darlan was murdered by a French boy who was shot within six hours after the admiral's death. Politically, the Darlan murder paid off, and got Franklin D. Roosevelt off an embarrassing spot. The inside story has not been told. The case of the missing British diplomats remains top line news.

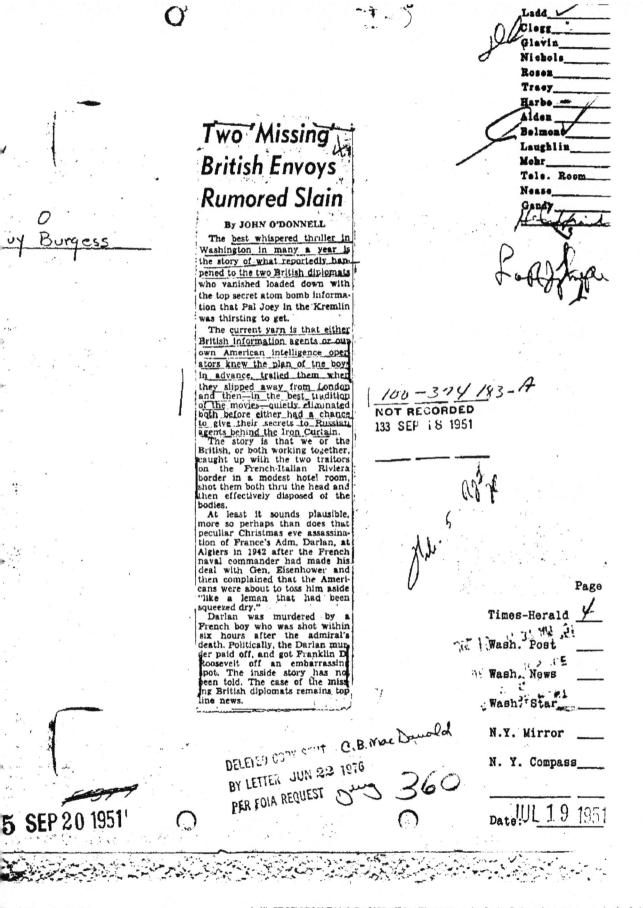

oy Burgess

Two Missing British Envoys Rumored Slain

By JOHN O'DONNELL

The best whispered thriller in Washington in many a year is the story of what reportedly happened to the two British diplomats who vanished loaded down with the top secret atom bomb information that Pal Joey in the Kremlin was thirsting to get.

The current yarn is that either British information agents or our own American intelligence operators knew the plan of the boys in advance, trailed them when they slipped away from London and then—in the best tradition of the movies—quietly eliminated both before either had a chance to give their secrets to Russian agents behind the Iron Curtain.

The story is that we or the British, or both working together, caught up with the two traitors on the French-Italian Riviera border in a modest hotel room, shot them both thru the head and then effectively disposed of the bodies.

At least it sounds plausible, more so perhaps than does that peculiar Christmas eve assassination of France's Adm. Darlan, at Algiers in 1942 after the French naval commander had made his deal with Gen. Eisenhower and then complained that the Americans were about to toss him aside "like a lemon that had been squeezed dry."

Darlan was murdered by a French boy who was shot within six hours after the admiral's death. Politically, the Darlan murder paid off, and got Franklin D. Roosevelt off an embarrassing spot. The inside story has not been told. The case of the missing British diplomats remains top line news.

100—374 183—A
NOT RECORDED
133 SEP 18 1951

Page

Times-Herald 4

Wash. Post

Wash. News

Wash. Star

N. Y. Mirror

N. Y. Compass

Date: JUL 19 1951

5 SEP 20 1951

Here Wilson 'ides' With Lab[or]

By Drew Pearson

DEFENSE MOBILIZER Charles E. Wilson has had many bitter battles with labor both before and after he came to Washington. However, the former General Electric boss pulled shoulder to shoulder with labor leaders last week in a closed-door assault on Congress for failing to pass effective price controls.

Wilson

More than 100 House members, including about 20 Republicans, heard Wilson, AFL President Bill Green and CIO Secretary-Treasurer James Carey denounce the badly gutted price control bill as a boon to Joe Stalin and an invitation to ruinous inflation.

"If the dollar goes down to 25 cents in value because Congress has failed to control prices, Joe Stalin will have gained a great victory without firing a shot," Wilson declared at the secret meeting, called by House Rules Chairman Adolph Sabath (D. Ill.).

"I do not agree with labor all the time, but I agree on this. We are moving into a period of stepped-up production for defense that will greatly increase the pressure on our economy. Yet Congress is about to pass legislation that weakens controls on inflation instead of stiffening them.

"I'm from big business and I'm proud of it," continued Wilson, "even though this spokesman for labor"—he pointed to CIO's Jim Carey—"has ripped into me from time to time in the past. But we've got to realize—all of us, business, labor, the farmer and Congress—that we must pull together unselfishly if we are going to win the battle against inflation."

Carey, Green and Charles Anderson, an official of the Railroad Brotherhoods, vigorously supported Wilson.

Missing Diplomats

In the background of the State Department's re-examination of 500 members of its staff from top to bottom, including the suspension of several career diplomats pending security hearings, was the mysterious disappearance of the two British diplomats.

This scrutiny is no reflection on any particular person, and any of those suspended merely face technical charges. The State Department, however, is taking precautions lest the same thing happen to the American diplomatic service that happened to the British. For, with the disappearance of the British career men, it was necessary to fly special couriers all over the world to change the secret codes of both the United States and Britain. In addition, almost every secret known to the two countries was potentially exposed to the Kremlin.

One of the most widespread and thorough manhunts in history has now been conducted for Donald MacLean and Guy Burgess. But so far every trail has led up a blind alley.

Every day that passes makes it more conclusive that MacLean and Burgess have disappeared behind the Iron Curtain—as was first predicted by the companion who started off with them and then came home.

Meanwhile here is the story of what happened, as intelligence officers have carefully pieced it together. It is a story illustrating the need for housecleaning all diplomatic deadwood before it is too late.

Asked to Leave

1. Before leaving the United States in May, Guy Burgess had become a diplomatic failure. Perhaps as a result, he had also become an outspoken anti-American. There is no record, however, that he engaged in any pro-Russian activities while in this country, but he had been asked to leave the United States because of drunken-driving and a strong protest by Virginia's Gov. John S. Battle.

2. MacLean was of a different calibre. Only 38 years old and son of a distinguished father, he was the chief of the American Division of the Foreign Office—a post in which he knew every vital Allied secret.

In recent years, however, MacLean had become increasingly unstable. Due to overwork he had two nervous breakdowns. He had also acquired a personality unbalance somewhat similar to Burgess', and his American wife was worried.

3. Before Burgess and MacLean left together for France on May 25, Burgess, the bachelor, told friends he was going to "visit the Continent" for several weeks. He was starting six weeks' leave from the Foreign Office, preparatory to looking for a new job.

MacLean, however, didn't have any official leave from his Government post. That Friday, when he left home, MacLean told his wife: "I'm going away for the weekend and will be back Sunday night or Monday morning."

Funds Believed Small

4. As far as the authorities can determine, neither man took more than a limited amount of money. Neither man is thought to have taken more than $200, though they could have hidden funds in their clothes, funds received in advance from the Russians.

5. Intelligence officers are certain that both Burgess and MacLean got as far as Paris. However, there's absolutely no record of their arrival or presence in the French Capital.

Copyright, 1951, by The Bell Syndicate, Inc.)

Page

Times-Herald ____
Wash. Post ____
Wash. News ____
Wash. Star ____
N.Y. Mirror ____
N.Y. Compass ____

Date JUL 17 1951

Officials Here Affirm

Missing British Official Knew Top A-Bomb Planning Secrets

By The Associated Press

Donald MacLean, the missing British diplomat, was a member of the committee that controlled the wartime exchange between this country and its partners in the development of the atomic bomb, a State Department spokesman said yesterday.

MacLean and Guy Burgess, a fellow British Foreign Office member, mysteriously disappeared from London May 25. They since have been the object of a broad international manhunt, accompanied by suggestions both may have slipped behind the Iron Curtain with vital secrets.

The State Department official here would confirm only that MacLean was a member of the combined policy committee that dealt with top-level international relations on the A-bomb project.

An article in United States News and World Report said MacLean knew "how many atomic bombs the West had, what were the uranium resources, how many bombs could be made with existing resources and materials."

The news magazine said MacLean did not know the scientific details, because the policy committee did not deal with them, but did know "the degree of atomic cooperation among the three countries — Great Britain, Canada, and the United States."

MacLean came to Washington as First Secretary of the British Embassy in 1944. In that post, the magazine said, important secrets passed through his hands. It said that when the top international policy committee on the atomic project was set up, he became secretary of the British section.

It added that another job was to arrange for "swapping facilities, exchanging scientists among the countries, for getting uranium and other materials, for dividing secrets."

"And it arranged for the admission of Dr. Klaus Fuchs into the United States," the article said. "There he got the atomic information that was to make him the super-spy of all time."

Fuchs now is in a British prison.

NOT RECORDED
42 SEP 26 1951

DELETED COPY SENT C. B. Mac Donald
BY LETTER JUN 22 1976
PER FOIA REQUEST

01 SEP 29

362

Vanished Diplomat's Atom Secrets Held of Little Value to Soviet

By the Associated Press

The State Department has disclosed that one of two missing British diplomats was in on atomic secrets that would once have been valuable to Russia. But it says they are probably of little value now.

The department said yesterday Donald MacLean was a British member, in 1947-48, of an American-British-Canadian policy committee on atomic matters.

MacLean and Guy Burgess, another British foreign office official, disappeared from London May 25, amid speculation they might have gone behind the Iron Curtain. An international manhunt has developed only fragmentary traces of them, so far as is known, in France.

The State Department spoke up on MacLean after the magazine U. S. News and World Report stated he knew "How many atomic bombs the West had, what were the uranium resources, how many bombs could be made with the existing resources and materials."

"Because of changes in the rate and scale of the United States (atomic) program" since 1948, a State Department spokesman said, "Information available to (MacLean) then would not be of any appreciable aid to Russia."

The department said MacLean had available to him information on patents, declassification matters and the research and development related to procurement of raw materials from foreign sources."

-A

363

Page

Times-Herald _____

Wash. Post _____

Wash. News _____

Wash. Star _____

N.Y. Mirror _____

N. Y. Compass _____

Date: JUL 17 1951

63 SEP 26 1951

State Dept. Concedes.

2 Britons Didn't Get A-Figures

By LYLE C. WILSON, United Press Staff Correspondent

The State Department sought today to knock down any ideas that a missing British diplomat knows how many atomic bombs the United States has or the process of making them.

The diplomt is Donald S. MacLean, 38. He and Guy F. Burgess, 40, disappeared from their British Foreign Office jobs on May 26.

The State Department concedes, however, that Mr. MacLean amassed a considerable amount of information on the U. S. atomic energy program. He got this information in 1947 and 1948 when he was secretary of the Combined Policy Committee which decided atomic matters for the U. S., Canada and Britain.

The State Department's explanation of Mr. MacLean's role in atomic affairs of the three nations was prompted by a copyright article in the magazine U. S. News & World Report.

TOOK JOB IN 1947

The magazine claimed Mr. MacLean "knew how many atomic bombs the West had, what were the uranium resources and how many bombs could be made with existing sources and materials."

The department pointed out Mr. MacLean assumed his job as secretary of the Policy Committee here February, 1947.

"Since 1946," the department said, "there has been no exchange of information concerning fissionable material production processes, weapons technology and developments or stockpiles of fissionable materials and weapons."

KNEW SOURCES

However, Mr. MacLean had information on the three nations' atomic patents for peacetime uses, amounts of uranium (the A-bomb ingredient) available to the three countries at that time and what the committee considered should be classified, or kept secret, in connection with atomic development.

Mr. MacLean   Mr. Burgess

"Some of the information available to him in 1947 and 1948," the department said, "was classified and would then have been useful at that time to the Soviet atomic energy program and strategic planners.

"Because of the changes in the rate and scale of the U. S. program in the intervening years, the information available to him then would not now be of any appreciable aid to the USSR."

The fact remains that Mr. MacLean and Mr. Burgess did compile a great deal of knowledge useful to the Soviet Union. Between them they also had knowledge of codes, of North Atlantic Treaty organization anti-Communist plans, Japanese peace treaty objectives and no telling what other information which they might have obtained outside their own areas of authority.

POLITICAL ISSUE

Disappearance of MacLean and Burgess on May 26 has become a hot political issue in Great Britain. Conservatives accuse the Socialist British government of negligence. The assumption from the moment of their flight from London has been that the two men fled behind the iron curtain.

Security experts here judge the British Socialists to be wholly unrealistic in their approach to Communist espionage. British security officials themselves and their organization get good marks. But it is suggested that the British government itself checks the vigor with which the British security organization might otherwise proceed.

63 SEP 26 1951

BY LETTER JUN 23 1976 MacDonald
PER FOIA REQUEST

1/CTO -37413-A
NOT RECORDED
42 SEP 22 1951

Page

Times-Herald ____

Wash. Post ____

Wash. News 6

Wash. Star ____

N.Y. Mirror ____

N. Y. Compass ____

364

Date: JUL 17 1_

Tolson
Ladd
Clegg
Glavin
Nichols
Rosen
Tracy
Harbo
Alden
Belmont
Laughlin
Mohr
Tele. Room
Nease
Gandy

Mr. Tolson
Mr. L.
Mr. Clegg
Mr. Glavin
Mr. Nichols
Mr. Rosen
Mr. Tracy
Mr. Egan
Mr. Alden
Mr. Belmont
Mr. Laughlin
Mr. Mohr
Tele. Room
Mr. Nease
Miss Gandy

Missing British Diplomat Knew Vital A-Secrets

Washington, D. C., July 16 (AP). —Donald MacLean, missing British diplomat, was a member of the committee which controlled wartime exchange between this country and its partners in developing the atom bomb, a State Department spokesman said today.

MacLean and Guy Burgess, fellow British Foreign Office official in London, dropped mysteriously from sight May 25. They have been the object of an international manhunt spurred by suggestions both may have slipped behind the Iron Curtain with vital secrets.

The State Department official confirmed only that MacLean was a member of the com-

Donald MacLean

bined policy committee which dealt with top-level international relations on the A-bomb project.

Handled Secrets.

He refused further comment on an article in U.S. News and World Report, which said MacLean knew "how many atomic bombs the West had, what were the uranium resources, how many bombs could be made with existing resources and materials."

MacLean came to Washington as first secretary of the British Embassy in 1944. In that post, the magazine commented, secrets passed through his hands. It said that when the top international policy committee on the atomic project was set up he became secretary of the British section. The policy committee once "arranged for the admission of Dr. Klaus Fuchs into the United States," the article said. "There he got the atomic information that was to make him the superspy of all time."

Fuchs now is serving a 14-year sentence in a British prison.

100-374183-A

NOT RECORDED
145 SEP 22 1951

365

ITL
CLAS 7 6 SEP 26 1951
From
NY   news
DATED JUL 17 1951
SEARCHED BY N. Y. DIVISION

MacLean A-Data Not Useful Now, State Dept. Says

By International News Service

The State department conceded today that missing British diplomat Donald MacLean once had access to vital atomic information, but contended it would be of little use to Russia now.

MacLean and a fellow British foreign office worker, Guy Burgess, disappeared from London May 25 under mysterious circumstances. A world-wide search has been unsuccessful and fears have been expressed that the pair may be in Russia.

A State department spokesman said that MacLean was made British secretary of the combined U. S., British and Canadian atomic policy committee in 1947.

Had 'Shared Information'

The spokesman emphasized, however, that this was a year after the United States banned the exchange of information about atomic weapons, fissionable materials and A-bomb stockpiles.

The spokesman stated:

"MacLean had opportunity to have access to information shared by the United States, Canada and the United Kingdom in the field of patents, declassification matters and the research and development of procurement of raw materials from foreign sources.

"In this capacity, McLean had access to information relating to estimates made in 1948 of uranium ore supplies from foreign sources available to the three governments for the period 1948-49 and the definition of scientific areas in which the three governments deemed technical co-operation could be accomplished with mutual benefit."

"Was Only Diplomat"

The spokesman said the scientific areas "in general" included such subjects as health and safety, research with low-power reactors, extraction chemistry, stable isotopes and radio-isotopes.

The spokesman added:

"The role that MacLean had in these activities was that of a diplomat. He is not a scientist and his duties in connection with combined policy committee matters was of a procedural and British diplomatic secretarial character.

"Some of the information available to him in 1947-48 was classified and would then have been useful at that time to the Soviet atomic energy program and to strategic planners.

"Because of the changes in the rate and scale of the U. S. program in the intervening years, the information available to him then would not now be of any appreciable aid to the Soviet."

Page

Times-Herald

Wash. Post _____

Wash. News _____

Wash. Star _____

N.Y. Mirror _____

N. Y. Compass _____

53 SEP 25 1951

Date: 7/17/51

ments or stockpiles of fissionable materials and weapons."

KNEW SOURCES

However, Mr. MacLean had information on the three nations' atomic patents for peacetime uses, amounts of uranium (the A-bomb's ingredient) available to the three countries at that time and what the committee considered should be classified, or kept secret, in connection with atomic development.

"Some of the information available to him in 1947 and 1948," the department said, "was classified and would then have been useful at that time to the Soviet atomic energy program and strategic planners."

"Because of the changes in the rate and scale of the U. S. program in the intervening years, the information available to him then would not now be of any appreciable aid to the USSR."

The fact remains that Mr. MacLean and Mr. Burgess did compile a great deal of knowledge useful to the Soviet Union. Between them they also had knowledge of codes, of North Atlantic Treaty organization anti-Communist plans, Japanese peace treaty objectives and no telling what other information which they might have obtained outside their own areas of authority.

POLITICAL ISSUE

Disappearance of MacLean and Burgess on May 26 has become a hot political issue in Great Britain. Conservatives accuse the Socialist British government of negligence. The assumption from the moment of their flight from London has been that the two men fled behind the iron curtain.

Security experts here judge the British Socialists to be wholly unrealistic in their approach to Communist espionage. British security officials themselves and their or-

State Dept. Contends:

2 Britons Didn't Get A-Figures

By LYLE C. WILSON United Press Staff Correspondent

The State Department sought today to knock down any ideas that a missing British diplomat knows how many atomic bombs the United States has or the process of making them.

The diplomt is Donald S. MacLean, 38. He and Guy F. Burgess, 40, disappeared from their British Foreign Office jobs on May 26.

The State Department concedes, however, that Mr. MacLean amassed a considerable amount of information on the U. S. atomic energy program. He got this information in 1947 and 1948 when he was secretary of the Combined Policy Committee which decided atomic matters for the U. S., Canada and Britain.

The State Department's explanation of Mr. MacLean's role in atomic affairs of the three nations was prompted by a copyright article in the magazine U. S. News & World Report.

Mr. MacLean   Mr. Burgess

TOOK JOB IN 1947

The magazine claimed Mr. MacLean "knew how many atomic bombs the West had, what were the uranium resources and how many bombs could be made with existing sources and materials."

The department pointed out Mr. MacLean assumed his job as secretary of the Policy Committee here in February, 1947.

"Since 1946," the department said, "there has been no exchange of information concerning fissionable material production, processes, weapons technology and developments or stockpiles of fissionable

ganization get good marks. But it is suggested that the British government, itself, checks the vigor with which the British security organization might otherwise proceed.

CPSIA information can be obtained at www.ICGtesting.com
Printed in the USA
BVOW09s0058310516

449819BV00035B/312/P